D1713647

WHY SOME THERAPIES DON'T WORK

Psychology Series

James A. Alcock, Ph.D., Series Editor

Other titles in the series:

ALBERT ELLIS, Ph.D.

and Raymond J. Yeager, Ph.D.

• •

WHY SOME THERAPIES DON'T WORK

• •

The Dangers of Transpersonal Psychology

 **Prometheus Books**

59 John Glenn Drive
Amherst, New York 14228-2197

Published 1989 by Prometheus Books

Inquiries should be addressed to
Prometheus Books
59 John Glenn Drive
Amherst, New York 14228–2197
VOICE: 716–691–0133, ext. 207
FAX: 716–564–2711
WWW.PROMETHEUSBOOKS.COM

Library of Congress Cataloging-in-Publication Data

Ellis, Albert, 1913–
    Why some therapies don't work : the dangers of transpersonal psychology / Albert Ellis and Raymond J. Yeager.
        p. cm.
    Includes bibliographical references.
    ISBN 0–87975–471–0
    1. Transpersonal psychotherapy—Evaluation. 2. Transpersonal psychology—Evaluation. I. Yeager, Raymond J. II. Title. III. Series: Psychology series (Buffalo, N.Y.) [DNLM: 1. Psychological Theory. 2. Psychotherapy. 3. Relgion and Psychology.

RC489.T75E44 1989
616.89'14

88–31809

Printed in the United States of America on acid-free paper

Contents

5

6   Contents

1

What Is Transpersonal Psychology and Psychotherapy?

Transpersonal psychology (TP) has become enormously and increasingly popular (and lucrative!) in the United States as well as abroad during the past fifteen years (Bordewich, 1988; Gordon, 1987; Lindsey, 1986b, 1987; Stevens, 1988). Thus, a questionnaire submitted to the readers of *Psychology Today* showed that "acceptance of the occult was high" (Bridgwater, 1984, p. 76). Eighty-three percent of the respondents believed in extrasensory perception; more than 50 percent believed in UFOs, faith-healing, and ghosts. Reincarnation was accepted by 47 percent.

Wiccans, or practitioners of witchcraft, are part of the broad neopagan movement, and one author puts the number of active neopagans at fifty- to one-hundred thousand. In the coven of one witch, Laurie Cabot, there are 2,000 members (Roelofsma, 1987).

A poll of one thousand college students revealed that 15 percent had faith in astrology, 30 percent believed in space aliens and the Lost Continent of Atlantis, and nearly 50 percent believed that the Bible stories of Adam and Eve and Noah's ark were literally true (*Free Mind*, 1987).

"Only spiritualists can buy or rent cottages on the 172-acre community known as Lilydale, a western New York Mecca for spiritualists—those who believe spirits live on after death and can be contacted by the living. Last July and August, forty thousand people attended group seances, private psychic meetings, demonstrations of psychic healing, and other spiritual activities" (B. Katz, 1985, p. 87).

According to sociologist, priest, and author, Andrew Greeley (1987), 42 percent of American adults now believe they have been in contact with someone who has died; 67 percent experienced ESP; 31 percent experienced clairvoyance; 73 percent believe in life after death; 68 percent believe that afterlife is Paradise; 48 percent had an unusual spiritual experience; 71 percent believe in heaven; 53 percent believe in hell; and 67 percent of teenagers believe in angels.

Harvard theologian Harvey Cox says that Americans are "mystically starved," and that is why they are flocking by the millions to "the born-agains, the hands-on healers, the charismatics, and now the out-of-body trippers like Shirley MacLaine" (Beware of Your Visions, Even Angels, 1987, p. 50).

In spite of the hordes that attest to its virtues and alleged effectiveness, the potential dangers of transpersonal philosophy and practice are great and increasingly predominant (Kurtz, 1986a). This book will discuss the potential as well as the current already harmful effects of transpersonal psychology and psychotherapy and will contrast them with the presumably more effective, realistic, and pragmatic approach of rational-emotive therapy (RET) (Ellis, 1957, 1962, 1973a, 1985, 1986a, 1987a, 1987b, 1988). As will be shown in chapter 2, RET is a pioneer school of cognitive-behavioral therapy, one of the most popular modes of contemporary psychotherapy, which rigorously attempts to be scientific and practical.

Transpersonal psychology covers a multitude of theories and methods and is often mistakenly considered to be identical to humanism or humanistic psychology. To clarify this misunderstanding, let us differentiate between the two. First, humanism has both psychological and ethical aspects. Psychologically, it involves the study of the whole person, has as its goals increasing long-term happiness and productivity, and encouraging self-actualization. Ethically, its interest is to help establish a set of guidelines by which humankind can responsibly and cooperatively live. The humanistic emphasis is on the interest and propagation of humankind, not on "inanimate nature, lower animals, or some assumed natural order or god" (Ellis, 1973a; p. 2). Any humanistically oriented psychotherapy will, therefore, include both psychological and ethical humanism. As will be discussed, transpersonal psychology and psychotherapy do not.

Transpersonal psychology (TP) includes many tenets, some of which clearly contradict those of humanism. Transpersonal psychology often believes and asserts that

1. Some higher form of consciousness exists which supposedly transcends normal human sensation and cognition (Ajaya, 1984; Ferguson, 1980; Franklyn, 1973; Krippner, 1986; Mann, 1984; Schneider, 1987; Walsh & Vaughan, 1988; Wilber, 1982a).

2. There are universal and all-encompassing forms of energy and light into which humans can tap and through which practically all physical and mental ills can be cured (Ajaya, 1984; All Together Now, 1985; Cardinal, 1986a; Ellis, 1979b; Mann, 1984; Krippner, 1986).

3. All living beings and inanimate things merge into one fundamental Unity. By understanding and blending with this undivided Oneness, men and women can overcome their human limitations; be in direct contact with God; eradicate all of their disturbances, distresses, and handicaps; and achieve boundless and eternal bliss (Anthony, Ecker & Wilber, 1987; Biela & Tobacyk, 1987; Bordewich, 1988; Drack, 1982; Ehrlich, 1986; Ellis, 1973a, 1973b; Franklyn, 1973; Hillman,

quoted in Goleman, 1985; Lindsey, 1986b; Nathanson, 1985; Questions and Answers on Basics, 1986; T. Roberts, 1982; Rogers, 1980).

4. Humankind is to surrender all sense of personal identity or ego and strive for a sense of egolessness, detachment, desirelessness, no-mind or Nirvana (Ellis, 1973a; May, 1986; Schneider, 1987; P. Russell, 1986).

5. Perfect knowledge, perfect peace, perfect joy, perfect unity with the universe, and perfect physical and mental well-being can be achieved by following transcendental teachings (Bordewich, 1988; Ehrlich, 1986; Harman, 1985; Lindsey, 1986b; Prabhupada, 1977; Schneider, 1987; Spirit Speaks, 1985).

6. God-like leaders, gurus, masters, and Holinesses are able to truly understand transcendental teachings and possess miraculous powers to magically and mystically diagnose and cure all ills (Bhatty, 1987; Clarke, 1988; Fisher, 1985; J. Gordon, 1987; Gruson, 1986b; Kaslow & Sussman, 1985; Lindsey, 1986a; Milne, 1987).

7. The Sacred Truth is revealed in holy scriptures such as the Bible, the Upanishads, the Kabala, and H. P. Blavatsky's *Secret Doctrine*. Transpersonal psychology often advocates that these scriptures be strictly and devoutly endorsed and followed (Franklyn, 1973; Luce & Hudak, 1986).

8. There exists a superhuman God or Supreme Being who rules the universe and whose acknowledgment and worship guarantee perfect and eternal enlightenment, peace, and happiness (Bartlett, 1985; May, 1986; Questions and Answers on Basics, 1986).

9. Paranormal experiences such as ESP, psychokinesis, astral projection, and psychic surgery indubitably exist and validate

transpersonal views and can be successfully used by adopting a transpersonal outlook (Emery, 1986; Ferguson, 1980; Kinzer, 1987; LeShan, 1984; Morain, 1988; Rogers, 1980; Wrobel, 1987).

10. Humans can create miracles and magical results by merely tapping into transcendental and higher sources of consciousness (Agena, 1983; Bartlett, 1985; Bhatty, 1987; Ferguson, 1980; Houston, 1982; Spirit Speaks, 1985; Suchman & Thetford, 1975).

11. The existence of afterlife experiences, reincarnation, and immortality of our souls has been empirically proven (Barron, 1987; Bhatty, 1987; Lindsey, 1987; J. Roberts, 1979; Schneider, 1987; Spirit Speaks, 1985; Venn, 1988; White, 1980).

12. Absolute Reality can be sought and found and, therefore, absolute, invariant, unchangeable, ineffable Truth can be reached (Ajami, 1986; Kurtz, 1985a, 1986a; Lewis, 1984; Questions and Answers on Basics, 1986; Radical Right Tills the Heartland, 1985).

13. Human beings are ruled by inexorable karma or fate and therefore often cannot decide their own destinies or make independent choices or decisions (Franklyn, 1973; Ohta, 1983; Schneider, 1987).

14. In addition to a body and a mind, human beings possess an ineffable and immortal soul or spirit whose disembodied essence will persist forever (Agena, 1983; Kinzer, 1987; Krippner, 1986; Ritscher, 1985; Spirit Speaks, 1985; Stace, 1960).

15. All humans possess a God within them that enables them to be perfect, to ward off harm, and to cure themselves miraculously of ills (Bugental, 1971; Lindsey, 1987).

16. We can understand the universe, and the mystical and magical

forces that exist in it, only through our personal experience and intuition. Objective and scientific knowledge, including that which explains or contradicts our personal and mystical intuition, is irrelevant or false (Bordewich, 1988; Bourne, 1986; Ehrlich, 1986; Ferguson, 1980; Rosicrucians, 1985; Shah, 1982; Stace, 1960; Tart, 1988; Tulku, 1977, 1978; Wilber, 1982a).

17. If we rigidly and compulsively follow religious and cultish rituals, we shall ward off evils and cure ourselves, often miraculously, of serious handicaps and ills (Ajaya, 1984; Bartlett, 1985; van den Hart, 1983; Weisman, 1986b).

18. The futures of individuals and groups can undoubtedly be read by resorting to astrology, fortune-telling, tarot-card reading, witchcraft, channeling, and other psychic methods. These can also be used to change one's future destiny (Abbas, 1986; Barron, 1987; Bufe, 1987; Kurtz, 1985a, 1986a; Rachleff, 1971; Rawcliffe, 1952; Regan, 1988; Rensberger, 1974; S. Roberts, 1988a, 1988b).

19. Disembodied spirits—such as astral projections, ghosts, and the spirits of long-dead sages—indubitably exist and can be consulted, through special mediums or other means, to guide our lives today (Agena, 1983; Franklyn, 1973; Kinzer, 1987; Krippner, 1986; Kurtz, 1986a; Ritscher, 1985; Spirit Speaks, 1985; White, 1987).

20. Many healing individuals—such as shamans, faith-healers, and saints—exist and undoubtedly have miraculous powers to cure us of virtually any disease or disability. It is not merely our *belief* in these healers that helps us overcome our affliction, but the real, superhuman powers that these special people (or objects or symbols) possess (Kinzer, 1987; Krippner, 1986; Rosicrucians, 1985; Stace, 1960).

21. There are many cults and authoritarian groups—such as the

Moonies, the Maharishi's Transcendental Meditation group, and the Rosicrucians—that promulgate mystical truths. If we become devout members of these groups and rigidly adhere to their rulings, we can achieve eternal bliss and avoid all ills (Fisher, 1985; Gordon, 1987; Lerner, 1986; Sullivan, 1988).

22. Altered states of consciousness—such as hypnotic trance states and biofeedback—exist and their existence proves that people have suprapersonal experiences; can go beyond their sensations, feelings, and thoughts; and truly have (and not merely *believe* that they have) transpersonal, mystical knowledge and actions. Altered states of consciousness also prove that humans have and can maximize superhuman, miraculous powers (Cowan, 1973; Ferguson, 1980; Franklyn, 1973; Houston, 1982; Tart, 1975, 1978; Walsh & Vaughan, 1988).

23. The fact that uncertainty exists (even physicists accept Heisenberg's principle of uncertainty) and that nothing is certain proves that many implausible transpersonal beliefs—such as devout beliefs in higher forms of consciousness and paranormal and afterlife experiences—are indubitably true (Ajaya, 1984; Capra, 1983; Ferguson, 1980; Grof & Grof, 1988; Mann, 1984).

24. That some people who believe in transcendental and supernatural phenomena sometimes derive benefits from these beliefs proves that such beliefs are valid (Ellis, 1973b, 1975a; Frank, 1975; Tart, 1988; Walsh & Vaughan, 1988).

25. Because some nonpsychotic (as well as many psychotic) individuals dogmatically believe in transcendental "experiences" and enjoy their beliefs and/or "experiences," these "experiences" themselves are "true" and prove the validity of transpersonal hypotheses (Ferguson, 1980).

26. Because birth is a very important part of life, because it is presumably the start of a new reincarnation, and because

the birth process itself allegedly leaves an indelible mark on people and their disturbances, the act of being born is sacred: rigid rituals in regard to birthing and rebirthing must be administered and observed. Otherwise, we will be warped and will lead a miserable, emotionally disturbed existence (Rowan, 1988).

27. Devils and demons, as well as gods and good spirits, definitely exist; therefore the understanding and placating of these satanic beings is necessary for the preservation of our life and health (Collins, 1986; Kinzer, 1987; Laurence, 1974; LaVey, 1972; Ritscher, 1985; Scott, 1970).

28. Because human desires inevitably lead to frustration and pain—which most of us just cannot bear—we should ideally strive for Nirvana or desirelessness, give up all ambition and competition, and attempt to achieve total calmness and perfect serenity (Chinese Garden of Serenity, 1976; Ellis, 1973a; Suzuki, Fromm & De Martino, 1963).

29. Since dying and death are important experiences and, presumably, a prelude to reincarnation, we must view them in a sacred light, dwell on them even when we are young, and go through compulsive rituals to make sure that we benefit from them (Gibbs, 1981; Rinpoche, 1986).

30. Because transpersonal views are sacrosanct and include the one and only Absolute Truth, and because enormous harm (such as Armageddon) will befall us if we ignore or oppose these transpersonal truths, we *must* completely believe in and follow them. If we don't, all true believers in transcendentalism have a perfect right to do anything—yes, anything!—to terrorize, torture, and annihilate us. Any kind of violence that they use to convert us or kill us is entirely legitimate. They will greatly benefit, especially in some kind of afterlife, if

transpersonal Absolute Truth is upheld via terrorism and homicide (Khomeini, 1985).

31. All humans have ineffable Being, which is beyond (transcends) their senses, thoughts, feelings, and behaviors and is the Ultimate Source of how they live and thrive. Although Being and Source are not observable or definable, they indubitably exist and may be reached and tapped through mystical (transcendental) intuition. Once our Being and Source are apprehended and tapped, we fully understand the Secret of It All and discover full efficiency and eternal bliss (Forum, 1985; Osborne & Baldwin, 1982; Tart, 1975; Wilber, 1982a, 1982b).

32. Our inner world is not only more important than the outer world or the "reality" around us but is also actually *more* real than other people and things with which we live. If we are truly in touch with this inner world, we can be perfectly happy no matter what goes on around us and can solve all our practical problems and avoid all evils (Wilber, 1982a, 1982b).

33. Right-brain thinking is particularly holistic and proves that transpersonal phenomena actually exist (Kinsbourne, 1982).

34. Meditation is not only a relaxing state that distracts us from our anxieties, but it is also a miraculous cure for practically all mental and physical ills (Ellis, 1984d; Hendlin, 1982; Kurtz, 1986a).

35. The visions and revelations of mystics are valid insights and prove that transpersonal theories are indubitably true (Sacks, 1985; Tart, 1975).

As we hope you can see, the tenets of transpersonal psychology are neither based on objective reality nor usually capable of experimental falsification. The view stems largely from Eastern as opposed to Western philosophy (Deikman, 1972, 1982; Ferguson, 1980; Mann, 1984); from various ancient Greek, Hebrew, and Middle Eastern mystics; from Hegelian philosophy; and from the transcendentalists of the 1840s, such as Ralph Waldo Emerson and Bronson Alcott, who introduced much of Asian philosophy to America. Its philosophical underpinnings are hardly scientific and its devotion to humanity is much in doubt. The distinction between humanism and transpersonal psychology is, therefore, fairly clear and will be discussed in detail later (May, 1986).

This text will compare and contrast the functional utility of transpersonal psychology with that of rational-emotive therapy. Rational-emotive therapy (RET) is a modern, humanistic school of psychotherapy that was first introduced in 1955 (Ellis, 1957, 1958) after my (A.E.'s) disillusionment with practicing psychoanalysis and with trying other modern forms of psychotherapy (Ellis, 1962). Although RET employs existential philosophy in its practice and conceptualization and involves some of the ideas of the ancient East— particularly those of Confucius and Buddha—it is mainly a Western, scientifically oriented form of psychotherapy. Most of its principles and practices are opposed to mysticism, occultism, transcendentalism, supernaturalism, and religiosity (Ellis, 1973a, 1980b, 1983b, 1983c, 1984d, 1985, 1986a, 1986b).

Rational-emotive therapy differs from transpersonal psychology and from its offshoot, transpersonal psychotherapy, in numerous ways. This text is devoted to discussing these differences in regard to their impact on psychotherapy and human life.

2

What Is Rational-Emotive Therapy?

Rational-emotive therapy (RET) was first introduced in 1955, subsequent to my (A.E.'s) general dissatisfaction with psychoanalysis and my discovery that my psychotherapy clients were not benefitting from getting "in touch" with unconscious motivations or "working through" transference reactions, as traditional psychoanalytic explanations maintain. Instead, clients changed as a function of changing the ways in which they perceived, interpreted, and evaluated themselves and their worlds. Hence, RET became a general school of psychotherapy focused on helping clients restructure their philosophic and behavioral styles.

In addition to discerning the vast importance of cognition in creating and maintaining human disturbance, I also observed that I could help people change through more time- and cost-efficient means. Rather than passively allowing clients to express their thoughts and feelings freely (or not so freely) and indirectly offering interpretations of the historical development of their disturbances, I introduced a more interactive, confrontative, and here-and-now direction to psychotherapy. I formulated what would become one of the most comprehensive and popular forms of psychotherapy ever (Bernard & DiGiuseppe, 1988; Corey, 1986a, 1986b; Gutsch, Sisemore & Williams, 1984; Heesacker, Heppner & Rogers, 1982; Smith, 1982; Weinrach, 1980; Wiener, 1988). The model of rational-emotive therapy, therefore, became one that emphasized the role of cognition in human disturbance and proceeded therapeutically in an active, directive, and systematic fashion in the here-and-now (Ellis, 1957, 1962, 1971, 1988; Ellis & Becker, 1982; Ellis & Dryden, 1987; Ellis & Grieger, 1986; Ellis & Harper, 1975; Hauck, 1973, 1974, 1975, 1979; Walen, DiGiuseppe & Wessler, 1980).

Whereas rational-emotive therapy primarily emphasizes the importance of cognition in human disturbance, it does not ignore biological, environmental, or cultural influences on human nature. On the contrary, RET asserts that such influences often constrain human potential for happiness and goal-production. Similarly, people often create spiritual constraints for themselves. However, although these constraints may often be present, RET emphasizes the innate capacity of humans to reconstruct their thinking and, therefore, redirect their lives.

Rational-emotive therapy, more than most forms of psychotherapy, seeks to help clients live with maximal amounts of happiness and productivity. However, people are not typically aware that their attitudes, emotions, and behaviors prevent them from achieving their goals. On the contrary, most of them often fallaciously believe their ways are functional and appropriate. The RET therapist, therefore, helps clients to restructure their beliefs about their emotional and behavioral problems.

Consider, for example, a client who experiences high degrees of anger at her husband. Typically, therapists quickly engage her in anger-management strategies, including relaxation processes and the like. However, if this client has a belief that her anger is functional or useful, no matter what the therapist does to minimize anger, he/she will likely be met with resistance. The client had better first agree that her anger is dysfunctional or counterproductive before she will be interested in working to give it up. The RET therapist, therefore, may first restructure the client's belief about the functional utility of her anger so that she will be more open to surrendering it (Ellis, 1976d, 1977a, 1984c, 1985, 1988).

Clients also typically believe that their emotions and behaviors are externally caused. RET therapists, therefore, work systematically to teach their clients that their emotions and behaviors are primarily the result of erroneous or irrational beliefs, and not the direct result of outside environmental or interpersonal events. Once clients accept that their beliefs are primarily responsible for their emotional and behavioral responses, then cognitive restructuring can more effectively be arranged.

Cognitive restructuring involves any process where a client's irrational beliefs and cognitive distortions are challenged, disputed, and restructured. This is generally done by having clients employ the hypothetical-deductive method of science whereby they (1) reformulate their absolutistic notions about the world into testable hypotheses, and (2) test these hypotheses. Those beliefs that can be reasonably and realistically supported with objective evidence will be kept and considered to be rational. Those beliefs that are unproven or are contradicted by existing evidence are given up. A new belief is, therefore, constructed (DiGiuseppe, 1986, Ellis, 1987b, 1987d, 1988; Rorer, 1988).

IRRATIONAL BELIEFS

There are numerous irrational beliefs that people may endorse that lead them to unnecessary and inappropriate levels of emotional distress. Let us examine four categories of irrational beliefs: (1) demand statements, (2) catastrophizing beliefs, (3) intolerance statements, and (4) rating statements.

Demand Statements. Statements of demand imply absolute necessity or need. People who make such demands essentially assert that they absolutely *must* have that which they *want*. They unyieldingly and rigidly dictate or command the way their worlds must operate.

They assert and believe that they, in fact, *require* that which they *desire,* as if they were the absolute rulers of the universe. People typic-ally demand approval, recognition, perfection, success, comfort, and a host of other things that are merely advantageous and preferable. However, the irrational demanding belief is evident when someone believes that he/she absolutely must have that which is likely *preferable.* The RET therapist, therefore, works to help clients restructure this belief that will likely lead to anger, intolerance, damnation, and other self-defeating emotional and behavioral states. The RET-er seeks to help people strongly desire only that which they believe they completely require (Ellis, 1985, 1987a, 1987b, 1987d, 1988; Ellis & Becker, 1982; Ellis & Dryden, 1987; Ellis & Harper, 1975).

Catastrophizing Beliefs. Catastrophizing occurs when people make "mountains out of molehills." Essentially, they magnify an event's badness and convert something that might realistically be considered a hassle into a horror. People also typically evaluate inconveniences as *awful* and pains as *tragedies.* The RET therapist works to help them restructure their tendencies to overevaluate something that is only bad, unfortunate, or undesirable (Ellis, 1957, 1962, 1988; Ellis & Harper, 1961).

Intolerance Statements. Irrational beliefs of intolerance exist when people strongly insist that they "can't stand" something or that it is "too" hard or difficult. People most commonly feel intolerant of frus-tration, discomfort, and other people. The RET therapist empathical-ly helps clients to modify their beliefs that life's frustrations and discomforts are unbearable or intolerable. Rather, they are helped to see such events as hard, but not *too* hard, and as difficult to stand but not *too* difficult or impossible (Ellis, 1957, 1977a, 1977b, 1977c, 1978, 1979a, 1979c, 1980a; 1981a; Ellis & Dryden, 1987; Ellis & Harper, 1975; Ellis & Knaus, 1977; Ellis & Whiteley, 1979).

Rating Statements. The irrational concept of rating involves mea-suring an individual's total human worth on the basis of some trait, behavior, accomplishment, or other attribute. The rational alternative is to help people to see that their human worth is independent of their actions or achievements. It makes no sense to say that one's value as a person is contingent upon any extrinsic measures. Yet, people tend to develop various equations as to what makes someone (or themselves) more or less worthwhile as a human (Ellis, 1962, 1972a, 1972b, 1973a, 1976b, 1979c, 1979d, 1984c, 1985, 1988; Ellis & Becker, 1982; Ellis & Harper, 1975).

Let us consider the belief that certain traits or "trophies" make people have more worth. We are not arguing that certain traits will not make you more valuable to do certain tasks. We are arguing that those traits do not make you a better person. Consider the belief that achievements make you more worthwhile. If this notion were true, that would mean that the second before the authors of this book earned our doctoral degrees, we had less human worth than we did one second after it was handed to us. Similarly, it would mean that my (R.Y.'s) human value was less one second before this book was published than it is after it is in print. Obviously, our intrinsic worth does not change. Only our credentials do.

In order for people to achieve happiness and maximize their productivity, it is important for them to restructure their irrational beliefs. According to RET, belief reconstruction is the primary means through which people make long-term therapeutic changes. Cognitive (as well as behavioral) modification can be employed to achieve many general goals of psychotherapy. We will now discuss some of the more common goals of personality change and discuss how RET and transpersonal psychology (TP) address these goals.

3

The Goals of Psychotherapy

Competing schools of psychotherapy can often be differentiated by examining the specific goals they have for their clients (Sundberg & Tyler, 1962). However, while different schools do have somewhat different specific goals, most share common general goals. For example, while client-centered psychotherapy (Rogers, 1961) strives to help the client to increase congruence between his/her real and ideal self, the Gestalt therapist is interested in helping clients finish unfinished business. Similarly, whereas the behavior therapist endorses a stimulus-response orientation, the cognitive therapist espouses stimulus-organism-response theory. However, despite these differences in focus, common treatment goals are shared. The cognitive therapist, the psychodynamic psychotherapist, the systems-oriented psychotherapist, and the transactional analyst also share common objectives. These commonly accepted goals typically include the following:

1. Achievement of a humanistic outlook

2. Advancement of scientific thinking

3. Achieving a profound philosophic change

4. Aiding self-acceptance

5. Increasing tolerance of others and a minimization of anger and damnation

6. Acceptance of probability and uncertainty

7. Increasing will and personal choice

8. Developing awareness and insight

9. Accepting human fallibility

10. Developing greater long-term hedonism and self-interest

11. Uprooting neurotic defenses

12. Achieving greater human freedom

13. Developing increased social interest

14. Abetting self-interest

15. Accepting the inevitable

We will now discuss these commonly accepted goals of psychotherapy and the different importance placed on each by both RET and transpersonal psychotherapy. We will also discuss how these goals are either facilitated or undermined by these two orientations.

4

How Transpersonal Psychology Is Antihumanistic

A primary goal of psychotherapy is to help people achieve a more humanistic outlook, that is, to help them to see that they are not entirely determined by forces outside of themselves, but to see that they also have the innate capacities for self-direction. Therefore, they had better realize that they do not "need" other people, supportive environments, or a "loving god" to determine their growth and destinies. It is also hoped that they will learn to live more cooperatively and constructively with other humans.

Rational-emotive therapy is frankly humanistic and expressly teaches its clients many of the principles of secular humanism (Ellis, 1962, 1972b, 1972c, 1973a, 1975a, 1977d, 1977e, 1980b, 1983a, 1983b, 1984a, 1984b, 1984c, 1985, 1987a, 1987c, 1987e, 1988; Ellis & Becker, 1982; Ellis & Dryden, 1987; Ellis & Grieger, 1986; Ellis & Harper, 1975; Ellis & Whiteley, 1979). It is humanistic in that it encourages individuals to develop their own identities and individualities more fully, but to do so while living in harmony with members of their social group. Rational-emotive therapy also cultivates a greater social interest, especially considering the destructiveness of nuclear-powered weaponry (Ellis, 1984b, 1984c, 1985, 1986a, 1987a). Though it considers human values primary, it does not encourage people to act selfishly and strive only for personal gratification. Greed and the demand that one's personal wishes be constantly fulfilled will likely lead to inter-personal and international conflict and disregard for world order. It may also lead to a rape of the land for short-term hedonistic reasons. Rational-emotive therapy stresses cooperation and encourages people to have a vital interest in preserving their environment.

While RET teaches people to cherish and protect lower forms of animal life and the ecology in which we live, it emphasizes human interests, including survival and happiness. For practical purposes, human interests are considered to be more important than the interests of inanimate objects and hypothetical gods. Humans are also somewhat more valuable than the birds and the bees and the flowers and the trees. Although "lower" animals are not considered sacred, they are still considered very important (and, of course, valuable to humans).

It is more functional and realistic to prioritize human happiness and survival over lower animals. To worship a cow and refuse to eat any flesh as the Hindus do, for example, or to choose the life of an animal over that of your own is dysfunctional and dangerous. Rational-emotive therapy and humanism would assert that animal sacrifice for *constructive* intentions is admissible since humans come first. This is not to allege that humans are intrinsically better than lower animals, but to contend that it is more functional for humans to prioritize their own survival.

Rational-emotive therapy does not advocate the senseless slaughter, harm, or exploitation of animals to abet human happiness. It does not endorse the slaughter of rare species of animals so that people may own a one-of-a-kind jacket or stole. Nor does it advocate hunting or trapping as a sport. Similarly, RET does not endorse or advocate the production of "milk-fed-veal," since these calves are raised in dark cages where they are *never* allowed to stand up so as to insure the tenderness of their meat. The killing and procurement of veal beef is based on the grandiose sense of human worth and a lack of consideration for other cohabitants on the planet.

Rational-emotive therapy does not support such a callously selfish attitude. Rather, it supports self-interest and the killing of animals for food or for potentially beneficial medical experimentation. This is not to say that all animal experimentation is done in ethical or responsible manners. Greater guidelines and monitoring of these experiments are needed. Generally, human importance is considered primary, but caution should be taken to prevent individuals from misinterpreting our "rank" as meaning that we need not care for lower animals.

The antihumanistic penchant of transpersonal psychology is evident when one considers its tendency to equate human importance with that of rocks and statues. Whereas humanism and, similarly, RET assign humans central importance, the transpersonal tendency is to equate human worth with that of other objects in the universe. Surely, if we are to improve our lives, we had better show greater concern for our planet's ecological condition. We also had better modify our disposal of wastes and plastics and utilize the world's resources more responsibly. We can also advantageously restructure what we consider to be our "needs." We often believe that we should be able to do whatever we desire, with little regard for ecological or environmental consequences. Some examples of this include our pathetic waste of energy and food resources.

In addition, although recycling programs are increasingly introduced, we waste much reusable material because of our low frustration-tolerance. We tend not to consider the long-term effects of our behaviors but find that conservation procedures are "too much trouble." Rational-emotive therapy works to help people think more responsibly and helps them see that, although it is difficult to sacrifice their short-term desires, it is often preferable to do so.

A humanistic emphasis, as is the case with RET, focuses centrally on humans; whereas, on the other hand, transpersonal psychology often focuses on the "sacredness" of all objects in the universe. It places the awareness of inanimate objects on a par with human consciousness. As Deikman (1972, p. 1) avers, "the awareness of a tree is not different from our own, it is continuous with it, like awareness is the origin of the entire system." Transpersonal psychology merges humans with inanimate "beings."

Another example of the antihumanistic stance of transpersonal psychology is its espousal of concepts such as egolessness, Nirvana, or selflessness. Transpersonal psychology advocates that humans completely and absolutely surrender personal desire and goal-seeking behavior and merge their identities with inanimate objects of the universe (Deikman, 1972, 1982; Mann, 1984; May, 1986; P. Russell, 1986; Schneider, 1987). Although RET challenges and points out the disadvantages of *rating* one's self or one's ego, it favors self-interest, productivity, and happiness. If people are without egos or an appreciation of being alive, enjoying and, to some extent, consciously directing their own destiny, they will not *choose* to live and to enjoy life. Egolessness doesn't abet human happiness or creativity. A catch-22 exists when an individual asserts, "I (ego) choose to remain egoless!"

Transpersonal psychology is also antihumanistic in that it often holds that humans must completely submit themselves to a supreme deity or Absolute (Bartlett, 1985; May, 1986). They must unquestioningly bow to this god's interests and whims, refusing to self-determine or to actualize their own concerns.

There is a failure among such believers to take responsibility for guiding themselves. Rather, they create and, it is presumed, devoutly follow arbitrary guidelines that are usually more rigid than is appropriate for the achievement of optimal human functioning. Followers of transpersonal psychology tend to believe that they are less than alive if they do not live up to these prescribed standards. They thereby invite passivity and lack of achievement.

Rational-emotive therapy, on the contrary, advocates self-direction and independence. It teaches people to accept themselves unconditionally, even if they do not behave exactly as prescribed by their leaders or gods. This attitude is similar to Christian teachings that assert that humans are always worthy even if they sin. They are ethically required to atone for their sins and make restitution, but they are, as humans, always forgivable and undamnable.

Transpersonal psychology paradoxically asserts that love and devotion to a god or higher level of consciousness make for intimacy with fellow humans. However, RET holds, supernatural beliefs handicap cooperation among people. To focus on suprahuman constructs and beings distracts people from taking care of business at home. As a result of devaluing their *own* worth, humans become less alive and less efficient. Rational-emotive therapy helps people become less dependent on supernatural events and more involved with inducing their own happiness.

Transpersonal psychology opposes the tenets of humanism in that it emphasizes living our lives on earth so that we may achieve happiness in an afterlife or heavenly existence (Barron, 1987; Bhatty, 1987; Lindsey, 1987; Schneider, 1987). This is likely to lead to numerous inter- and intrapersonal problems. People become obsessively directed toward "ultimate rewards," thereby unreasonably depriving themselves during their mortal lifetimes. They opt for sacrifice, asceticism, and martyrdom, thus sabotaging their here-and-now pleasures. Although it is beneficial for society to become more future-oriented, and while it would benefit from a greater long-term hedonistic position, the transpersonal attitude of deferring happiness until a "greater" afterlife reward can be secured not only endorses the improbable but is also dysfunctional and depression producing in the one lifetime we have for sure.

Transpersonal philosophy also fosters some of the worst kinds of antihuman censorship, oppression, fascism, violence, terrorism, religious war, and genocide—all fanatically perpetuated in the name of some authoritarian supreme power who commands that his or her zealous followers subjugate and destroy their opponents and thereby achieve satisfaction in a conjectured heaven (see chapter 8). For example, consider the violence that currently exists in Ireland. Both the Irish Protestants and Catholics believe in the same God and believe in Jesus Christ as the Son of God and Messiah. Although they are reasonably congruent in their general ideologies and philosophies, they are engaged in a brutal protracted war connected with seemingly trivial details and practices of their religions. This is a case where each sect's dogmatic adherence to their ways and beliefs leads to rabid intolerance. Although Jesus presumably taught his followers to turn the other cheek and accept thy brother, as a result of many Irish people's dogmatic adherence to "Christian" principles, Jesus' messages are lost and contradicted. As is often true, devoutness leads to serious functional impairment. The devout belief that "you *must* follow *my* God and must follow God *my way*," together with "I must convince you," continually foments religious conflicts.

The transpersonal orientation also denigrates human consciousness in favor of the alleged achievement of "Divine Consciousness" (Ajaya, 1984; Emmett, 1973; Mann, 1984; Schneider, 1987; Wilber, 1982a). Transpersonalists assert that through a higher level of consciousness you will learn to "save yourself." Higher consciousness is also used as a way to slyly convince you that you can or will become perfect. By encouraging people to become obsessed with achieving perfection, transpersonal psychologists help people to be dissatisfied with themselves and their lives (Bordewich, 1988; Ehrlich, 1986; Harman, 1985; Lindsey, 1987; Schneider, 1987; Spirit Speaks, 1985).

Transpersonalists claim that by achieving Nirvana or Total One-ness, you are *by definition* perfect. There is obviously no way to falsify this belief. Such tautological and empirically unfalsifiable reasoning is common among transpersonal thinkers (Bordewich, 1988; Drach, 1982; Ehrlich, 1986; Lindsey, 1986b; Popper, 1985; Roberts, 1982).

Those who seek perfection usually believe that one *must* achieve this perfect state since it is so highly desirable, and that one must *continue* to achieve it, thus bringing on almost inevitable anxiety. The *demand* for perfection is, therefore, a target for rational inter-vention.

Another example of how TP diverges from a humanistic outlook can be observed in its typical pleading for the achievement of "ultimate values" and "ultimate meaning" (Granger, 1972), of absolute perfection, and faultless truth (Ajami, 1986; Capra, 1983; Ferguson, 1980; Kurtz, 1985a, 1986a; Lewis, 1984). These concepts, like many others espoused by transpersonal thinkers, are vague and imprecise. As Popper (1985) argues, constructs like these cannot be falsified and are therefore tautological or definitional. Humanism, in contrast, is highly practical and pragmatic.

Within the transpersonal realm, there also exists an obsession with superhuman, subhuman, and nonhuman entities. This obsession denigrates the importance of what is uniquely and distinctly human. The word "transpersonal" essentially means "beyond the person" or "beyond humanness." It delves beyond that which is human to what may be considered to be "superhuman." Transpersonalists reach beyond plain sensation and experience into the mystical and metaphysical. They essentially go beyond that which is real.

In reaching beyond the tangible, transpersonalists refuse to accept reality as we know it. They deny that the universe is basically impartial and resist the idea that magical phenomena are contradicted by empirical observation. They adopt a polyannaish, unrealistic outlook, believing (often devoutly) that powers actually exist that are greater than those with which humans are realistically endowed. Transpersonalists refuse to accept reality for what it is and prefer to pursue an a illusion of extra-humanness that they have created (Agena, 1983; Bartlett, 1985; Bhatty, 1987b; Spirit Speaks, 1985). A rational-emotive perspective encourages humans to accept reality and human limitations fully and not to fall victim to illusions of grandiose afterlife promises.

A primary goal of TP is to achieve what Bugental (1971, p. 34) calls the search for the hidden god within ourselves: "to be aware about this primal fact of [our] immediate being without preconception, self direction, or social/interpersonal apprehension." But this is the essence of what Lasch (1978) calls the evils of the me generation: autistic self-absorption to the point of shutting out other humans (Schneider, 1987). Humans uniquely are immersed in cultural and social mores, in preconceptions and conceptions, in self-direction and interpersonal concerns. If Bugental and his fellow transpersonal therapists had their way, they would help to dehumanize, decerebrate, and desocialize us earthlings—and to render us much less humanistic.

We humans typically want answers and, when we do not quickly receive those we want, we tend to make them up ourselves. We have a unique and innate tendency to create structure for ourselves as a result of our refusal to accept doubt or uncertainty. Because reality is replete with uncertainty, and since we will not accept this and demand that we "have all the answers," we often refuse to accept reality (Capra, 1983; Ferguson, 1980; Grof & Grof, 1984; Mann, 1984). Instead, we invent religions and "higher orders" to satisfy our perceived *need* for an ultimate meaning in life.

Human beings would likely be better off if life and reality were accepted for what they are: uncertain, often unfair, temporary situations that are terminable. If we were to accept this perspective, we would not need to reframe our trials and tribulations as examples of God's higher plan. Although this rationalizing (not rational) attitude may help us cope with some of life's distresses, if we were to accept unfairness as something tolerable and often inevitable, we would cope even better. Our tendency to read hidden meaning into life's events exacerbates our somewhat paranoid outlook about the world's "overwhelming dangers." Transpersonal psychology enhances this kind of paranoid thinking.

In terms of advancing a humanistic outlook, transpersonal psychology and psychotherapy signally fail. Whereas they profess to be humanistic, their theories and practices do not reflect such an orientation. Rational-emotive therapy, on the other hand, is clearly humanistic, both psychologically and ethically.

5

Sabotaging Scientific Thinking

A second major general goal of psychotherapy is to advance scientific thinking. That is, clients are helped to perceive, interpret, and evaluate their worlds more objectively, realistically, and constructively. The scientific perspective facilitates this by favoring nondogmatic and flexible thinking, where hypotheses are formed and checked against empirically derived data. The client/scientist tries to falsify his/her hypotheses and thereby revise them. Theories are, therefore, open-minded and flexible, logico-empirical, hypothetical-deductive, and always subject to revision. According to Popper (1985), a hypothesis must provide the criteria for its own falsification; if not it leads to unresolvable argument. If it is not falsifiable it may be "true" under all conditions—which, of course, is ludicrous.

Perhaps more than any other major school of psychotherapy, rational-emotive therapy endorses a scientific model and utilizes it in several key ways (DiGiuseppe, 1986; Ellis, 1962, 1973a, 1983b, 1987a, 1987e, 1988; Ellis & Dryden, 1987; Rorer, 1988). Transpersonal psychology, however, is highly unscientific. In fact, the transpersonal perspective seems to be the very essence of antiscientism.

Transpersonal psychology often ignores hypothesis testing as a means to uncover truth. Whereas the rational-emotive perspective and the scientific model consider an individual's beliefs to be merely his/her hypotheses about life events, the transpersonal view considers these beliefs to be either truths or falsehoods without ever testing them. Propositions are "validated" not on their being supported by empirical evidence, but by the fact that they uphold the transpersonal theory. Whereas a scientific model tests hypotheses either to support or disconfirm a theory, the transpersonal model uses theory to support or dispute an individual hypothesis or belief. It is, therefore, irrelevant whether a belief is empirically supported or not. Rather, it is supported if, and only if, it makes sense in terms of transpersonal philosophy. Some of the antiscientific characteristics of TP will now be discussed.

Transpersonal psychology is dogmatic in its contentions, and often asserts that it knows the ABSOLUTE TRUTH (Ajami, 1986; Colodzin, 1983; Ferguson, 1980; Kurtz, 1986a; Lewis, 1984; Mann, 1984; Stace, 1960). It does not view its assertions or beliefs as hypotheses but instead dogmatically and irrevocably considers them to be valid. It frequently dictates that the universe follows *one* universal law, which is based on ABSOLUTE or God-like TRUTH, into which humans can always tap and find direction and answers. Transpersonal psychology asserts that this TRUTH always existed and will forever and unyieldingly exist.

Transpersonalists dictate three main Truths: (1) God does in fact exist and humans must follow Him and His rules to achieve earthly and heavenly rewards. (2) There are invariant right and wrong ways to behave. (3) Absolute goodness and absolute badness exist and lead to heaven and hell (Nathanson, 1985). All of humankind *must* not only devoutly believe but also follow these dogmatic "truths."

The absolutistic, demanding, and nonscientific transpersonal view typically demands perfection and adherence to rigid prescriptions for human behavior; any variation of this prescription leads to damnation and persecution. There is little room for human error, fallibility, creativity, uniqueness, or individuality. The guidelines are present and must be strictly followed. Divergence is, therefore, sinful and punishable.

The strictness and inflexible attitude of TP clearly contradicts the scientific outlook and that which is presented in parts of the New Testament. In the New Testament, Jesus reinterprets the Ten Commandments as a set of guidelines by which humans can choose to direct their lives. Humans are, therefore, encouraged to follow these guidelines but are not damned to hell for failing to do so. The Christian view is that humans are fallible, and it is only rational to expect them to err in their attempts to live cooperatively and follow their God. Christian forgiveness offers a less rigid, although still not highly scientific, view of human behavior.

The rigid doctrines of TP lead to debilitating effects. As a result of its stifling demands, an increased probability of human disturbance follows. Whereas science allows alternative rules of behavior, transpersonalism often presents only one absolute.

Transpersonal psychology eschews experimental analyses and favors subjective experiences over more objective means of data collection. It also deifies the acquisition of knowledge through pure intuition rather than through empirical examination (Bourne, 1986; Ehrlich, 1986; Gertrude Enelow, cited in Colodzin, 1983; Ferguson, 1980; Mann, 1984; Shah, 1982; Tulku, 1977, 1978). A scientific attitude, as included in RET, uses direct observation as its primary source of data and seeks more objective knowledge (while recognizing that no knowledge is *purely* objective [DiGiuseppe, 1986; Kuhn, 1970]). Although intuition and opinion may lead us to generate interesting and useful hypotheses, "truth" includes some relationship to empirical findings. However, transpersonalism posits truth apart from reality testing.

Transpersonal emphases also tend to distort our views of the nonhuman world by anthropomorphically and fanatically endowing it with consciousness and other human qualities (Bertrand Russell, cited in Brink, 1984). We are not concerned with anthropomorphic similes that are commonly used in the English language, since discussing the "hands" of a clock or the "eye" of a hurricane will hardly lead to human disturbance or interpersonal conflict. We do, however, challenge the belief that statues or logos, for example, have supernatural powers. Such a perspective is often paranoid. Endorsing such a belief will likely lead humans to neglect their abilities to direct their own destinies and to surrender their will to some falsely endowed idol.

Similarly, transpersonalists rely on charismatic gurus and supposedly divine leaders for direction, revelation, and truth (Bhatty, 1987; Clarke, 1988; Fisher, 1985; Gordon, 1987; Gruson, 1986; Kaslow & Sussman, 1985; Levine, 1984; Lindsey, 1986a; Milne, 1987). This tendency often serves to increase dependency needs, decrease self-confidence and self-efficacy, and lead to an identity disturbance.

The anthropomorphic view of transpersonalism also holds that other objects in the universe—such as a tree, lamp, or table—also have feelings and awareness. This view is, at best, unprovable and potentially debilitating. First, there is no evidence whatsoever to support the "hypothesis" that such objects possess an "ego" or experience anything. Why would one chose to believe in a hypothesis that is so devoid of any empirical support? Second, to endow objects with humanlike qualities places humans on a par with these objects in terms of value and priority for survival. As mentioned earlier, this is hardly a functional or helpful belief.

The transpersonal view is also antiscientific in that it directly contradicts observed reality and alleges, for example, that "there are no physical limitations to inner vision . . . the psychic faculties of man know no barriers of space or time" (Rosicrucians, 1984, p. 32). Transpersonal psychology also insists on the unity of total cosmic reality and refuses to separate analyzable aspects of living organisms and inanimate objects, as does science (Tannous, 1983).

Transpersonal psychology directly combats scientific teachings. For example, it often holds that fundamentalist and creationist views are as valid as the more widely accepted scientific theories (Mormon Professor Faces Furor, 1984). Transpersonalists deny the data regarding evolution and the development of the cosmos obtained through paleontology, anthropology, and paleoanthropology. Instead, they attribute evolution to God. The transpersonal argument is based not on data but rather on tautology. It uses single assumptions to "validate" innumerable points despite having no data to support these assumptions. Its monolithic TRUTHS are used to combat all counter-arguments.

Transpersonal psychology is also antiscientific in that it endorses many other "phenomena" despite having no data to confirm them as valid. In spite of scientific failure to confirm telepathy, precognition, psychokinesis, clairvoyance, fortune-telling, out-of-body phenomena, psychic surgery, exorcism, ghosts, and monsters, transpersonalists often devoutly and unqualifiedly uphold their existence (Abbas, 1986; Barron, 1987; Bhatty, 1985, 1987; Boyd, 1988; Braude, 1986; Cardinal, 1986b; Culver & Ianna, 1984; Emery, 1986; Flew, 1987; Fuller, 1980; Gardner, 1987; Goldberg, 1988; H. Gordon, 1987, 1988; Hines, 1987; Howell, 1988; Hunt & McMahon, 1985; Keller, 1988; Kurtz, 1985a, 1986a; LeShan, 1984; Lester, Thinschmidt & Trautman, 1987; MacDougall, 1983; Montgomery, 1985; Randi, *USA Today,* 1986; Rensberger, 1974; Rice, 1980; S. Roberts, 1988a, 1988b; Rogers, 1980; Shelburne, 1987).

The antiscientific nature of the belief in and "experiences" of psychic phenomena are steadily outlined in the outstanding publication *The Skeptical Inquirer.** Some articles on this subject appearing in recent issues of this journal include those by Blackmore (1987), Dean (1987), Dennett, (1985), Emery, (1988), Flew (1986), Kurtz et al. (1988); Rotton (1985), and Sagan (1987).

Transpersonal psychology tends to cling religiously to anecdotal reports as supporting data for psychic "phenomena." Also, it often confuses correlational with causal relationships. For example, many individuals tend to conclude falsely that they "had a bad day" because they walked under a ladder that morning. Or, they believe that a black cat crossing their path will actually cause bad fortune. Although these and many other similar examples are obviously superstitions,

---

*P.O. Box 229, Buffalo, New York 14215–0229

transpersonal believers will conclude quite differently. They tend to infer a particular conclusion in the absence of any supporting data.

Transpersonal psychology also claims that knowledge of some of the most important aspects of reality is "attainable *only* by means of mystical insight" (Griffin, 1984, p. 116), thereby dismissing the functional import of scientific methodology. Transpersonalists argue that mystical insight is real knowledge and all other knowledge is only temporary (Sacks, 1985). Science, too, asserts that all knowledge is temporary, since it considers its findings to be forever challengable and ever-changing and not undying truth. Rather, it views knowledge as revisable and does not, therefore, entertain ultimate truths. The hypothesis that mystical insights may in fact be valid is entertained by a scientific perspective. However, the view's lack of falsifiability and its current failure to be supported by empirically derived data render it improbable.

Transpersonalists avow that Absolute Truth is self-experienced and cannot be disproven by empirical data or by logical analysis (Bordewich, 1988; Ehrlich, 1986; Ferguson, 1980; Mann, 1984; Rosicrucians, 1985; Shah, 1982; Tulku, 1977, 1978; Wilber, 1982a). This assertion serves as a protective blanket against any scientific scrutiny: for example, that by definition Absolute Truth is untestable.

Transpersonal psychology employs vague, undefined, and overgeneralized terminology that is often tautological and therefore cannot be proven or disproven. To have practical value, a theory should use understandable, rather than esoteric, terminology. Concepts such as *allness* (Korzybski, 1933), *oneness, truth, being, karma, and Nirvana* are incompatible with sound scientific investigations. Such constructs are hardly tied to observables that in some final analysis, are prerequisites of science. Similarly, transpersonalists continually resort to definitional and circular statements, such as Hegel's statement about "Spirit's discovery of Spirit as Spirit" (cited in Wilber, 1982c), that contain no empirical referents but are widely accepted as indubitable truths.

Transpersonal psychology also persistently and stoutly posits unfalsifiable hypotheses that cannot possibly be scientifically checked (Popper, 1985). It is almost devoid of one of the main ingredients of science, namely, a fiercely skeptical tendency to scrutinize (Read, 1983). Transpersonalists take their beliefs as facts, without ever challenging them against observed or measurable reality. Essentially, since they "make sense" in terms of their vague theories, they wrongly conclude that their positions are, in fact, accurate.

One means through which transpersonalists preserve their beliefs as "facts" is through tautological reasoning. Through this process they argue by definition and confuse cause and effect. For example, consider Deikman (1982, p. 6): "The fundamental source of individual being . . . is beyond ordinary awareness; mystics call it the Self or Truth or Knowledge."

Transpersonalists argue against science, asserting that scientific or objective thinking prevents humans from finding the true essence of things. They continually excoriate science as "materialistic," "technological," "superficial," "mechanical," and "soulless" (Bhatty, 1983). Transpersonal psychology also claims that "pure" knowledge is knowledge that is totally devoid of any sensory, cognitive, or empirical elements. But, such knowledge can be experienced or known (Willard Quine, cited in Read, 1983).

Another example illustrating transpersonal psychology's opposition to science is its tendency to utilize pseudoscientific arguments. For example, one favorite claim is that since modern physics includes the Heisenberg principle of uncertainty as well as Einstein's theory of relativity, Absolute Unity exists and (highly improbable) magical beliefs and superstitions are also valid (Capra, 1983; Ferguson, 1980; Houston, 1982; Kurtz, 1986a). Hoaxes, as in the case of Castaneda's mystical writings about the teachings of Don Juan—a sorcerer who actually never existed (de Mille, 1976, 1980, 1981)—Uri Geller's disproved bending of spoons (Krippner, 1984), and unproven claims of psychic surgery are also endorsed. The transpersonal view is that since something cannot be absolutely or totally disproven, it therefore exists. Although this *may* be so (because unlikely events like psychic surgery *can* be true when they most probably aren't), transpersonal psychologists argue that phenomena that have not been totally disproven indubitably *do* exist. Their use of *non sequiturs* and tautologies are, therefore, ubiquitous.

Another very important phenomenon also occurs. Charlatanism is exceptionally rife in transpersonalism. Knowing the great gullibility of many people, and wanting to capitalize on it to gain fame, fortune, and power, literally thousands of charlatans create mystical and magical "events" and palm those off as real. Harry Houdini (1924), for example, investigated mediums who tried to dupe him by supposedly talking to his beloved dead mother; he spent considerable time and money unmasking them. He and several other magicians have offered to pay ten thousand dollars or more to any medium whose tricks they cannot duplicate with their regular magic; so far not a single legitimate medium has shown up to claim these rewards. James Randi, the magician, along with the Buffalo-based Committee for the Scientific Investigation of Claims of the Paranormal, under the chairmanship of Paul Kurtz, actively carry on antihoaxing research projects today.

Various investigations over a period of many years have consistently found transpersonal devotees resorting to fraud and deception. Thus, Arthur Wrobel (1987) has compiled many articles on *Pseudo-science and Society in 19th Century America.* Jeffrey Mishlove (1983), in a revision of his 1980 Ph.D. dissertation for a doctorate in parapsychology from the University of California at Berkeley, has acknowledged "the actual faking of psychic events" (pp. 140–141). James S. Gordon (1987) shows what a con man Bhagwan Shree Rajneesh was and how unscrupulous were some of his chief associates. Lloyd Morain (1988) has shown some of the rudiments of flimflammery to be found in occultists. Willis Harman (1985) foolishly maintains that safe fire-walking is a matter of mind over matter, when in fact it is well-known that simple physical principles are involved in this stunt (Dennett, 1985; Leikind & McCarthy, 1985).

Kendrick Frazier (1986) has edited a second volume from *The Skeptical Inquirer* whose articles, a reviewer notes, "document the unreplicable results, unreliable records, uncontrolled experiments, unsupported claims, and downright hoaxes that have characterized claims of the paranormal" (Pinker, 1987, p. 107).

"Psychic diagnosis" exercises have been used by *est,* Silva Mind Control, and other transpersonal groups presumably to show participants that they possess ESP. Actually they are set up so that participants "are given a good bit of help by the laws of chance, their suggestibility, and hints from the person administering the process" (Applebaum, 1979).

"Scientific" investigations of extrasensory perception (ESP) are often faked by outwardly dishonest or honestly misled experimenters. Boyce Rensberger (1974, p. 14) reports on one of the most notorious of ESP frauds:

> The effort of scientists to demonstrate the existence of extrasensory perception (ESP) and other so-called psychic phenomena suffered what many observers consider a serious setback recently when it was discovered that the director of one of the best known parapsychology research centers had been falsifying his experimental data.
>
> Until the deception was detected by the scientist's colleagues last June and admitted by the scientist, his findings had been regarded as among the most exciting of the scientifically reputable attempts to show that psychic phenomena exist.
>
> Parapsychology is the study of alleged mental powers such as mental telepathy and clairvoyance that cannot be accounted for within the present limits of understanding how the mind works. Many psychologists contend that evidence that such powers exist is lacking.

Seeking Distance

The disclosure comes at a time when legitimate parapsychology researchers are struggling to maintain their distance from what is sometimes called "the occult explosion"—the booming popular interest in astrology;

witchcraft; demonic possession; figures such as Uri Geller, the Israeli entertainer; and assorted nonscientific pursuits such as communication with living plants and dead people.

The discredited experiments had strongly suggested that rats could influence the workings of a self-contained electromechanical device simply by willing it mentally.

Faith-healing is one of the most important aspects of fundamentalist and transpersonal psychotherapy. We shall discuss this subject more fully in chapter 15. Here, however, is Paul Kurtz's (1986b, p. 5) summary of some of the articles in the Summer 1986 issue of *Free Inquiry* that show how much fakery and dishonesty exists in the work of some of the most popular contemporary faith-healers:

In this issue of *Free Inquiry,* we continue our exposé of the so-called faith-healers. A team of researchers, sponsored by the Committee for the Scientific Examination of Religion and led by special investigator James Randi, has uncovered a shocking tale of trickery and deceit on the part of some faith-healers who have used their religious authority to mislead millions of people. Our inquiry, which began seven months ago, has now involved over sixty volunteers and has sent teams of investigators into faith-healing meetings in such far-flung cities as Rochester, Brooklyn, Houston, Stockton, Anaheim, Sacramento, San Francisco, Philadelphia, Detroit, St. Louis, and Ft. Lauderdale.

What we have uncovered is the clever use of deception by some TV evangelists who claim that they are receiving messages from God. The faith-healer walks up and down the aisles of an auditorium that is jam-packed with sick, crippled, and even dying people. He calls out a person's name, makes his way to that person, and identifies his or her affliction, often giving the subject's address, and in many cases he gives the name of the doctor. The evangelist then, amidst prayerful thanks to Jesus, proclaims the healing process. Those in the audience are so impressed by this word of knowledge that they break into applause. The subjects are so overwhelmed that they often break into tears. No illness is considered too serious by the evangelist to be cured: Broken bones, cancer, heart disease, epilepsy, emphysema, diabetes, pneumonia, deafness, and blindness are healed. Spinal columns are reconstructed and blood transfusions are administered instantaneously. Moreover, the faith-healer implores the people in the audience to throw away their canes, crutches, and wheelchairs—and in some cases even their medications.

How does the evangelist obtain his "word of knowledge"? Does he receive it directly from God? Is he psychic? Does he have special mental powers? In the Spring issue of *Free Inquiry,* James Randi reported that W. V. Grant claimed he received divinely inspired messages, yet we discovered that Grant used crib sheets and a mentalist's memory act. He had obtained prior knowledge about the person who came to be healed: either from letters written to him or from information gleaned earlier in the evening by Grant or his confederates.

We now have new and incontrovertible evidence that Peter Popoff receives secret radio transmissions from backstage. We have confirmed the fact that Popoff—perhaps the most flamboyant of the TV evangelists—has a small receiver inserted in his ear. The so-called messages from God are really messages from Mrs. Popoff backstage. This cruel hoax is being perpetrated on helpless and innocent people who are waiting for divine deliverance. The details of these messages and how they were obtained are in the following articles by James Randi, Steven Schafersman, and Robert Steiner. We have skillfully planted "healees" in the audience at services given by Popoff, Grant, David Paul, and others in order to determine how the evangelists derive their information. Moreover, we have documentation of the charges made in this issue, including taped recordings and videotapes of the proceedings.

Other reports of fraud, lying, and charlatanism in regard to the occurrence of "psychic" phenomena are almost innumerable. Some recent exposés in this area include those by Booth (1986), Busch (1987), Emery (1987, 1988), Flew (1987), Frazier (1987), Gardner (1981), H. Gordon (1987), Hansel (1980), Houdini and Dunninger (1947), Klass (1986), Kurtz (1985a, 1986a, 1986b, 1986c; Kurtz et al, 1988); Nickell (1987), Rachleff (1971), and Rawcliffe (1952). Constant updates in this area are published in *The Skeptical Inquirer.*

As a result of their distaste for scientific or realistic reasoning, transpersonal psychologists remove psychotherapy from the realm of science and encourage their clients to take guidance not from observed reality or rational thinking, but rather from their intuitive minds and from other intangible sources with names like "higher mind, spiritual guidance, deeper self, God, collective unconscious, Universal Intelligence, or Divine Self" (E. Brown, 1984, p. 18). They often assert that you should tap into the world's universal energy, as do devotees of the Silva Mind Control Method (Silva & Miehle, 1977). Or, as devotees of the even more rational religions advise, you can find peace, relaxation, and salvation through prayer. Transpersonal psychologists dismiss alternative hypotheses, which explain how the behaviors of praying can induce relaxation and increased concentration. They also dismiss biological explanations for phenomena such as faith-healing (Levinthal, 1983). Rather, advocates of transpersonal approaches rigidly opt for their own explanations, dismissing other hypotheses as off base and uninformed.

As can be seen above, transpersonal psychology opposes the scientific model in many meaningful and significant ways. Most transpersonalists honestly believe in the psychic phenomena they supposedly experience—including astral projection, extrasensory perception, encounters with people from outer space, and past-life experiences. Many of these devout believers are psychotic, but most are probably neurotically deluded. Wishing very strongly to have supernatural experiences, they creatively manage to have them.

6

Blocking Profound Philosophical Therapeutic Change

A third goal of psychotherapy is to help its people achieve profound philosophical changes. Rather than helping clients to merely get through difficult life circumstances or to employ palliative strategies to conquer difficult emotional states, psychotherapists seek to help them perceive, interpret, evaluate, and interact with their environments differently in order to increase their long-term happiness and productivity. Psychotherapists seek to assist their clients to develop more realistic and functional views of their worlds, thereby reducing their inflexible, rigid, dogmatic, and maladaptive patterns. Rational-emotive therapy specifically and deliberately addresses these issues, attempting to help clients rid themselves of their pervasive self-defeating, irrational, and unrealistic ways of conceptualizing their worlds.

Rational-emotive therapy assumes that there are many means or techniques through which people help themselves to change their destructive life philosophies, with and without therapy. It asserts, however, that the most elegant, thorough, and comprehensive personality modification is achieved by making profound philosophical or attitudinal change and particularly by surrendering absolutistic demands. Irrational beliefs are thereby restructured to facilitate people's staying with strong desires and preferences and refraining from advancing rigid demands. Whereas transpersonal psychology espouses dogmatic reasoning, rational-emotive therapy encourages clients to look for open and alternative-based solutions. The rational-emotive therapist also shows clients how their beliefs are largely responsible for their neurotic disturbances, how absolutistic beliefs are usually counterproductive, and how clients can modify their irrational beliefs by applying scientifically based interventions.

Transpersonal psychology agrees with the rational-emotive perspective that cognitive change frequently leads to personality change. The cognitions transpersonalists suggest be changed, however, usually deal with the acceptance of God or some other "Higher Power." They claim that clients cannot achieve "real" happiness without this particular kind of thinking (Bartlett, 1985; May, 1986; Questions on Basics, 1986). Although they do endorse cognitive change as a prerequisite for emotional and personality change, they tend to address only one supranormal belief. Rational-emotive therapy argues instead that this is an inelegant way of changing. Unlike TP, RET helps clients change their general irrational and philosophic demands and their basic cognitive inflexibility and rigidity.

In addition to presenting unscientifically verifiable beliefs presumably to secure long-term personality change, transpersonal psychologists also present inelegant methods as solutions. For example, they offer strategies such as giving up one's identity or becoming attached to the Absolute and to other spiritual dogmas (Pennachio, 1983). In addition, transpersonal psychology enthusiastically endorses such methods as prayer, ESP, faith-healing, and exorcism as emotionally curative (E. Brown, 1984; Caddy, 1984a, 1984b; Dart, 1984; Ellis, 1972c, 1973b, 1977e, 1985, 1986b; Harper, 1983; Houston, 1982; Malcolm, 1984; Ray & Lehrman, 1984; Wolkomir, 1984; also see chapter 15). Rational-emotive therapists, however, view these transpersonally oriented forms of interventions as largely palliative measures. In addition, they may also prove iatrogenic and actually cause harm or treatment setbacks.

There are drastic differences between RET and TP in helping clients make philosophical changes. Whereas both forms of psychotherapy argue that profound philosophic change is preferable, the beliefs targeted in each therapy are quite different. Rational-emotive therapy seeks general philosophic change aimed at helping clients think in more scientific and humanistic terms. Transpersonal psychology, on the other hand, seeks to help clients think less empirically and base their perceptions more on intuition rather than on science or observed reality. Rational-emotive therapy tries to help clients minimize the extent to which they place demands on themselves, others, and the world, and to learn to accept themselves and others unconditionally—whether or not they perform well or badly. The transpersonal view is, in some ways, diametrically opposed.

7

Interfering with
Unconditional Self-Acceptance

Increased self-acceptance is one of the more commonly held treatment goals of various schools of psychology. However, rational-emotive therapy, along with Carl Rogers's (1961) client-centered approach, is one of the few popular therapies that promulgates and teaches unconditional self-acceptance. Other schools teach conditional self-acceptance or self-esteem instead (Branden, 1984).

Rational-emotive therapy shows people how to accept themselves fully (1) independently of whether they possess preferred accomplishments or traits; (2) independently of whether others (including their therapists) approve, respect, or love them; and (3) only on the condition that they *choose* to acknowledge and accept themselves and not on the basis of any external conditions (Ellis, 1962, 1971, 1972b, 1973a, 1976b, 1987a, 1988).

Whereas RET definitely does not endorse unconditional acceptance of people's *behavior,* it encourages unconditional *self*-acceptance. That is, the client presumably would not want to choose to engage in behaviors that are self-, other-, or society-defeating. Rather, he/she would prefer *not* to continue defeating or unproductive behavior.

However, refusing to accept one's *behaviors* is very different from refusing to accept one's *self*. The person wants to learn from his/her "sins" or transgressions and make atonements and corrections. The client does not, however, benefit from condemning his/her *self* for such errors.

The transpersonal emphasis, on the other hand, often asserts strict conditions under which the client is considered acceptable. If his/her behavior, values, and ideas are not within TP's realm of acceptability, the entire person is also outside of this realm. Transpersonal psychology's penchant is to appraise behaviors and censure people because of its appraisals!

Transpersonal psychology often asserts that people can only really accept themselves if and when

1. They achieve so-called Higher Consciousness.

2. They acknowledge and worship some God or Supreme Being.

3. They merge with the universe and achieve complete Unity with all inanimate matter and living things.

4. They reach a state of mindlessness, detachment, or Nirvana.

5. They behave well in their present life so that they will be properly reincarnated in future existences.

6. They rigidly conform to the teachings of some deified charismatic leader or guru (Capra, 1983; Deikman, 1972, 1982; Ferguson, 1980; Mann, 1984; Stace, 1960).

Clearly, in terms of their respective notions of self-acceptance, rational-emotive therapy and transpersonal psychology are often opposed. Rational-emotive therapy avers unconditional acceptance whereas transpersonal psychology is usually strictly conditional.

Despite assessing people as "worthy" only if certain criteria are met, transpersonalists often disagree about these criteria. Thus, whereas sects like that of Rajneesh make a person more "worthy" if he/she has free sex, other transpersonal groups rate people highly in terms of their virginity or abstinence. If one's value as a human depends on following certain behaviors, might the person not expect to have one consistent guideline for all to follow? Transpersonalists are highly inconsistent in this respect.

Some transpersonal psychologists teach people that they can only achieve goodness, worth, or acceptance by not having a self or personal identity at all. Acceptance, therefore, is achievable only through reliance or dependence on external things or conditions. For example, followers of transpersonal psychology may only be allowed to accept themselves fully by believing in the grace of some God or Absolute. However, and paradoxically, TP fails to inform them that they themselves actually *choose* to have this devout belief and thereby *choose* self-acceptance through a hypothetical intervening variable (such as God or Unity) that they *choose* to create.

Transpersonal psychologists also usually fail to teach their clients or followers to realize that they actually (1) choose to be devout, (2) choose to accept (or reject) themselves, and (3) choose the hypothetical conditions by which they deem themselves acceptable.

Transpersonal devotees often believe that they absolutely must be devout or else they are no good. In other words, by believing in TP they choose to give themselves little choice!

The concept of unconditional self- and other-acceptance is intrinsic to rational-emotive therapy, which clearly differs with transpersonal psychology on this point: TP mainly offers acceptance only by highly conditional means. Whereas unconditional acceptance allows people to correct and atone for their "sins" and limitations and to feel regret, concern, and sorrow when they act foolishly, accepting their selves conditionally predisposes them to unnecessary anxiety, self-deprecation, and depression—all of which may prevent them from learning from their own or others' mistakes.

Although transpersonal psychology ostensibly at times advocates self-reflection and self-control, it actually fosters considerable dependency and exceptionally conditional self-acceptance. As K. Fisher (1985, p. 22) has noted:

> Manipulative groups control information to limit alternative choices, denigrate critical thinking, define the outside world as evil, insist that a person's distress is due to lack of belief in the group and can be relieved by conformity, induce physical or psychological debilitation through fasting or fatigue, and encouraging trancelike states through chanting, hypnosis, or guided imagery.

8

Increasing Hostility, Damnation, and Terrorism

Probably one of the most important goals of psychotherapy, one that is likely to enhance social living is to help people to tolerate and minimize their hostility toward and damnation of others. To some extent, this goal is shared by rational-emotive and transpersonal psychotherapists. However, for the most part, RET and TP significantly differ in this respect.

Transpersonal psychology sometimes teaches forgiveness and grace, mainly through its devotees identifying with the Absolute, with God, or with one of His sons or prophets. However, despite sometimes articulating a highly forgiving and understanding emphasis, in some ways transpersonalists actually foster unforgiveness, intolerance, and damnation of others. Like any creed that is highly sectarian, that professes to know the Ultimate Truth, that relies on pure intuition, and that cannot be scientifically verified or falsified, transpersonal psychology has a tendency to foster one-sided religiosity, fanaticism, and dogma, often resulting in extreme segregation, bigotry, and violence.

Rational-emotive therapy specializes in teaching people to increase their tolerance of others and to remove bigotry and damnation. It is one of the few current psychotherapies that emphasizes the grandiose and disturbed nature of anger and intolerance and encourages the minimization and surrender of hostile and enraged feelings (Bard, 1980; Ellis, 1962, 1973a, 1977a, 1983b, 1984a, 1984c, 1985, 1987a, 1987c, 1987e, 1988; Ellis & Dryden, 1987; Ellis & Harper, 1975; Grieger & Boyd, 1980; Grieger & Grieger, 1982; Hauck, 1974; Walen, DiGiuseppe & Wessler, 1980; Wessler & Wessler, 1980). Rational-emotive therapy asserts that as soon as one believes in an Absolute Truth and believes that everyone must categorically share this belief, one will tend to feel prejudice, bias, and anger against other people (Ellis, 1983b).

Rational-emotive philosophy ardently endorses unconditional acceptance of differences in opinion. People are not damned for their views, even if these views are not shared or understood. Clients, therefore, need not agree with opposing viewpoints. Rather, the goal of RET is to help them accept the fact that different people often do have different outlooks and that this is acceptable and tolerable. Even if people endorse a philosophy that is apparently misinformed or dysfunctional (as we view transpersonal philosophy), RET tries to help the client accept *them* (but not their *philosophy*). If clients see their own outlook as being productive, appropriate, and realistic, they can view the opinions and theories of others as irrational while still rationally allowing these people to have them.

Although many mystical and devout sects of the transpersonal movement are actually peace loving, humane, and accepting of others, many other factions are quite authoritarian, politically rebellious, nonaccepting, and even warlike. These latter fanatically oriented religious groups have instigated a large number of violent acts, such as the child-beating practice of several fundamentalist Christian sects, which includes public displays of whipping in the streets (Clendinin, 1984a, 1984b; Bible Is Cited, 1984; Smothers, 1988). Also, several cults, such as the Neo-American church, have been accused of sexually abusing children in religious rituals.

"Hundreds of pictures showing sexual abuse of children were found in Harrisburg, Pennsylvania, the police said 'when investigating this cult' " (Inmate Said to Head Cult Mixing Sex and Religion, p. A13).

Many other examples of violent outbursts have been perpetrated by fundamentalist religious and transpersonal groups, including these:

Couer d'Alene, Idaho—Duane Hagadone, a millionaire resort and newspaper owner, says the future of northern Idaho is dynamite. He's referring to the economic prospects of the area but, given four bombings here since mid-September, his choice of words is ominous.

Located in the state's heavily timbered, lightly populated panhandle, the area's fertile soil makes it the USA's largest producer of Kentucky bluegrass. But there's another type of seed—one imported and planted in the early '70s—that has been harvesting this idyllic mountain community national attention.

The seed is hate and it has been watered by the Church of Jesus Christ Christian (Aryan Nations), an avowed white supremacist sect with headquarters in Hayden Lake, 15 miles north of here.

Three men and a woman—all with ties to the church—were arrested in connection with the bombings, which federal prosecutors say were part of a plan to intimidate opposition and begin a new race war. (Yates, 1986)

——— • ———

Riverhead, L.I., New York, April 9—A witness to the drug-induced killing of Gary Lauwers testified today that the defendant, James Troiano, had told a companion to slash Mr. Lauwers's throat as he pleaded on hands and knees for his life.

Speaking in a monotone punctuated by occasional sobs, the witness, Albert Quinones, said Mr. Lauwers had offered his assailants $500 to spare his life and later tried to escape.

But Mr. Lauwers was then kicked and beaten, the 17-year-old witness said, forced to declare his love for Satan and finally killed in a ritualistic frenzy last summer.

Mr. Quinones said Mr. Troiano, 19, and his companion, Richard

Kasso, 21, had persuaded Mr. Lauwers to accompany them to a small clearing in a dense woods in Northport. He said the assailants had used remnants of the victim's clothing to light a campfire.

An Attempt to Escape

"After they cut Gary's hair," he said, "Gary Lauwers got up and Ricky jumped on Gary's back and hit him in the neck and bit him in the ear and then Ricky stabbed Gary in the side and then Gary ran into the woods."

"Ricky grabbed Gary by his jacket and he brought him back to the campfire," said Mr. Quinones, a junior at Kings Park High School. "Jimmy picked up the knife and gave it to Ricky and then Ricky made Gary get on his knees and say, 'I love Satan.' "

"Jimmy was telling Ricky to slice his throat," Mr. Quinones said, adding that Mr. Troiano had repeatedly drawn his forefinger across his windpipe in a cutting motion.

"Then Gary said, 'I love Satan.' " (Gruson, 1985)

———— • ————

Mountain Home, Ark., April 25—The men of the Covenant, the Sword and the Arm of the Lord, mostly bearded, talk quietly, smile often and are friendly even to strangers. They are affectionate, hugging each other and dangling babies on their laps. There are lots of babies. Where an earlier generation might have exclaimed, "Oh, wow," the Covenant people say "Praise the Lord!" and they say it often.

But when asked if they believe that Jews are the offspring of Satan, Kerry Noble, the leader of the Covenant, which is the political and paramilitary arm of the church of Zarepath-Horeb, says simply, "Yes, we believe that."

And should all "racial Jews," in Mr. Noble's terminology, be eliminated?

"Not at this point," Mr. Noble replies. "In the future, I think all of you who are Aryans are going to wake up to the truth and whatever action you take is your choice."

Anti-Semitic Link Seen

Mr. Noble, an affable man with a slow, bright smile, was interviewed at a motel here where members of the sect were housed after a heavily armed force of up to 300 state and Federal officers peacefully took control Monday of the 224-acre Covenant camp in the Ozark mountains near here after a four-day standoff.

The Covenant is only one of the extreme right-wing groups under investigation by the Federal Bureau of Investigation. The links among the groups, which investigators say continue to emerge, are not so much organizational as religious, based on the violently anti-Semitic teachings of sects referred to collectively as the Christian Identity Movement. They hold that Jews are the offspring of Satan, and, according to the most extreme doctrine, should be exterminated.

Inside the rough-hewn Covenant camp, searchers found an arsenal that included submachine guns, grenades, an antitank rocket, plastic explosives, and a quantity of other explosives. (King, 1985)

Terrorism, torture, and other forms of violence are of course not restricted to mystical and religious groups, as a considerable amount of such violence has social, racial, and political origins. However, when racists and politicians form extremist groups that resort to terrorist and fascist tactics, they frequently tie up with devout religionists and transpersonalists. Thus, Louis Farrakhan, an American rabble-rouser, in one of his fascistic tirades, "talked about how good he looked, how he should be compared to Jesus, how the Jews were after him, how he was on a divine mission" (Crouch, 1985, p. 23).

Again, we read about two white American racist groups:

Seattle, Wash., Dec. 30 (UPI)—Nine men and a woman accused of conspiring to bring about a racist revolution were convicted today on racketeering charges based on a cross-country crime spree by a white supremacy sect called the Order.

Prosecutors said the group committed crimes from Philadelphia to California to finance its efforts to create an Aryan homeland and eliminate blacks, Jews and "white traitors."

The defendants were among 23 members of the Order accused last April in a wide-ranging racketeering indictment of involvement in two murders, robberies that netted more than $4 million, counterfeiting, weapons violations, and arson. (Ten Rascists Are Convicted of Racketeering Charged by Seattle Jury, *New York Times*, Dec. 31, 1985, p. A7)

———— • ————

Washington, Mo., May 18—A law enforcement official said today that a Missouri man who is accused of plotting to kill the Rev. Jesse Jackson made a statement to an informer implying that others had done the high-level planning.

The accused man, Londell Williams, 30 years old, a self-described member of a violent neo-Nazi terrorist group, and his wife, Tammy J. Williams, 27, have been charged in a Federal complaint with conspiring to kill or injure Mr. Jackson, the Democratic Presidential candidate; with possessing an unregistered automatic weapon, and with threatening to kill an informer in the case.

No others have been arrested, but Federal officials said the investigation was continuing and evidence would be presented to a Federal grand jury.

A Secret Service agent testified at a hearing Tuesday that agents had tape-recorded a conversation between Mr. Williams and an informer in which the suspect said the neo-Nazi group was planning to kill Mr. Jackson. The anti-black and anti-Semitic group calls itself the Covenant, the Sword and the Arm of the Lord, and is sometimes known as the C.S.A. (King, 1988)

The foregoing items tend to show that religious and racial-political fanaticism often go together. As I (A. E.) pointed out in my pamphlet *The Case Against Religiosity*, secular and religious devoutness and intolerance are birds of a feather and tend to foment the same kind of social evils (Ellis, 1983b).

Not all cult groups, of course, advocate or resort to violence, and some are quite pacifist. But absolute devotion to sects and their supreme leaders often arouses great wrath against dissenters, and violence easily goes with such wrath. Sect leaders themselves, moreover, sometimes get so carried away with the power that their followers give them that the leaders themselves resort to encouraging terrorist acts. Note, in this respect, the following items:

Wheeling, W. Va., Sept. 17 (AP)—The leader of a Hare Krishna community and a follower who is serving a life sentence for murder have been indicted on charges of burning a building to collect $40,000 in insurance.

Kirtanananda Swami Bhaktipada, head of the 700-member community at New Vrindaban, and Thomas Drescher, convicted last year of killing a sect member, were charged with three other followers in three Federal indictments made public Wednesday, said United States Attorney William Kolibash.

The charges against Mr. Bhaktipada, referred to in the indictment by his former name, Keith Hamm, and Mr. Drescher include one count each of conspiracy to commit mail fraud and arson, illegal use of fire or explosives, and malicious destruction, Mr. Kolibash said.

'Script Is Fresh'

West Virginia's Hare Krishna community, one of the largest in the nation, has been the subject of controversy since it was created in the 1960s. Investigators have been looking into allegations, including child abuse at the 4,000-acre community. (Two in Sect Charged in Insurance Case, *New York Times*, Sept. 18, 1987, p. B5)

— • —

Rajneeshpuram, Ore., Sept. 30 (AP)—Followers of Bhagwan Shree Rajneesh sang and danced around a bonfire tonight as they burned about 5,000 copies of the sect's former holy book and the robes of the guru's former secretary.

The books and the flowing red robes of the former aide, Ma Anand Sheela, who abruptly left the commune about two weeks ago, were heaped onto four wooden pallets covered with flowers and juniper branches.

The ceremony, in the community's crematorium, was part of the guru's

announced intention to repudiate ideas and projects that he says were
conceived by Miss Sheela, who left with about a dozen other top officials.

The 53-year-old guru has accused Miss Sheela of heading a gang that
committed crimes ranging from attempted murder to arson. His disciples
say they have dismantled an elaborate electronic eavesdropping network
that included bugs in the guru's bedroom. (Guru's Book Is Burned at Oregon
Commune, *New York Times*, Oct. 1, 1985, p. A15)

——— • ———

1982 to 1985 newspapers and networks breathlessly followed the
incredible developments in Rajneeshpuram (formerly Antelope), Oregon:
the ingathering of tens of thousands of orange-clad followers; their mortal struggle with the local ranchers and retirees; the trials convicting
Rajneesh leaders of fraud, attempted murder, mass poisoning, immi-
gration violations, and numerous lesser crimes. Frances FitzGerald of
The New Yorker compiled the definitive journalistic account. (Benderly,
1988)

Eleanor Grant (1988) reviews *L. Ron Hubbard: Messiah or
Madman?* by Bent Corydon and L. Ron Hubbard, Jr. (1988):

Messiah or Madman? is less a coherent account of L. Ron Hubbard's
life than a catalogue of cultish horrors: the bizarre Sea Org, a fleet
of Scientology-run ships where "Ron's" word is law, mischievous children are locked away in damp cabins and disobedience results in food
or sleep deprivation; the harrassment and framing of those who seek
to leave the church or expose its darker side; and Hubbard himself,
bigamist and opium addict, surrounded by nubile teenage "messengers,"
plotting to destroy the World Federation of Mental Health and to bug
and burglarize the Internal Revenue Service.

Robert Lindsey (1986a) comments on L. Ron Hubbard:

In the late 1960s, he decided to move his headquarters offshore to a
large yacht, the Apollo. He also declared that Scientology was a religion.

But by 1975, facing increasing legal attacks abroad and denied admission to port after port, he returned to the United States and established new headquarters in Clearwater, Fla., and in southern California.

In this period, according to court documents, the Church of Scientology began a project in which members of an elite group were assigned to infiltrate government agencies in more than 30 countries and suppress investigations of the organization.

The documents allege that members used confidential data gleaned in the "auditing" sessions, often involving sexual and other sensitive subjects, to intimidate potential dissidents.

Thousands of documents seized in 1978 by agents of the Federal Bureau of Investigation in a raid at Scientology offices here indicated that the church had conducted a far-ranging intelligence operation against more than 100 government agencies in this country. The bureau said the organization had carried out burglaries, wire-tapping, and theft of government documents.

In 1979, Mary Sue Hubbard, Mr. Hubbard's wife, and 10 other Scientologists were convicted of burglarizing and wire-tapping government agencies that church leaders said had harassed the church for decades.

—— • ——

Los Angeles, Jan. 1 (AP)—More than 400 current and former members of the Church of Scientology have filed a $1 billion lawsuit against the church, accusing it of trying to compromise or pay off two Florida judges and siphon $100 million to foreign bank accounts.

The suit, filed Wednesday by Lawrence Levy, a lawyer, contends that church officials or their representatives committed fraud and breached fiduciary duties. It says information obtained in purportedly confidential "auditing" sessions with a lie detector-like device was used "for purposes of blackmail and extortion."

The suit seeks an injunction and $1 billion in punitive damages, plus unspecified general damages. (Church of Scientology Is Sued for $1 Billion, *New York Times*, January 2, 1987, D14)

—— • ——

Washington, D.C., Feb. 9—A Federal district judge today dismissed

62   Why Some Therapies Don't Work

the Synanon organization's claim to tax-exempt status as a drug reha-
bilitation program and religious group, ruling that it had engaged in
systematic fraud against the court.

In dismissing Synanon's appeal to regain the tax benefit, Judge
Charles R. Richey said the California-based group had engaged in "will-
ful, systematic and extensive destruction and alteration of documents
and tapes" needed to assess its right to the exemption.

Judge Richey said his dismissal was based on the group's "egregious
misconduct," amounting to a "scheme to interfere with the judicial ma-
chinery."

"Chilling Portrait" Created

The judge also found that the group's own records and transcripts of
statements by its leaders "raise serious questions concerning Synanon's
financial operations and create a chilling portrait of an organization
that advocates terror and violence."

Judge Richey said that Synanon's founder, Charles Dederich, had
warned in a 1977 speech: "Don't mess with us. You can get killed dead.
Physically dead."

Mr. Dederich and two other members were later convicted of
conspiracy to murder a lawyer who had filed suit against the group
on behalf of two former members. The lawyer was bitten by a rattlesnake
when he reached into his mailbox. (Werner, 1984, p. A12)

As May (1986), Kurtz (1986a), Schneider (1987), and other critics
of transpersonal and mystical psychology have pointed out, there is
often a fine line between TP and dogmatic religion. Transpersonalists almost always describe themselves as "spiritual" or "religious"—
and it is exceptionally difficult to distinguish between these two terms.
More importantly, devout transpersonalists and devout religionists are
often almost identical in their absolutistic beliefs; and both groups
(if, indeed, they are two) have a strong tendency to promote, or at
least excuse, violence, torture, terrorism, and wars directed against
their dissenters and opponents.

Religious wars and terrorism have been rife since biblical times as Franklin Ford (1985) shows in *From Tyrannicide to Terrorism.* Reviewing Ford's book, Weber (1985) notes:

> On the way, we encounter prototypes of modern terrorists—the Israelite Zealots of the first century, terrifying all who differed from their murderous fundamentalism; the radical Muslim schismatics, who 10 centuries later, formed the sect of the Assassins and learned to do well by doing harm, using the terror they inspired to extort funds that subsidized further terror. Zealots and Assassins were murderously certain about the moral rightness of their cause, as their successors have been in the European religious wars of the 16th and 17th centuries or our age's national and social struggles.

In our own day, there has been no surcease of religious wars and terrorism. For example, religious violence has recently been rife in Afghanistan (Kifner, 1988), Cameroon (C. May, 1984a.), Nigeria (C. May, 1984b), India (Hazarika, 1984; 35 Reported Killed in New India Riots, 1984; Weisman, 1986a, 1986b, 1988), Ireland (Clines, 1986), Lebanon (Friedman, 1984a, 1984b; Hijazi, 1986a, 1986b, 1988), Israel (Skutel, 1984), the Philippines (Wren, 1986), Iran and Iraq (MacKenzie, 1986; Safavi, 1986), and in Malaysia (Crossette, 1986). Numerous other extreme cases of political oppression, terrorism, blackmail, breaking and entering, and general acts of violence during the past decade also mark the violent preoccupations of many transpersonal factions.

One of the more infamous of the devout and violent religious leaders in the world is the Ayatollah Khomeini. In Iran, Khomeini has established a state religion and opponents of his regime are jailed, tortured, and killed for disagreeing with the state philosophy. For similar reasons, Khomeini and his devotees have waged suicidal and genocidal wars against other nations and have aggressively tried to politicize and religionize the people of other countries (Friedman, 1984b; T. Smith, 1984).

Khomeini made a profound statement on religious war and terrorism in a 1984 address marking the birthday of the Islamic prophet, Mohammed. As quoted in the April 1985 issue of Harper's magazine, Khomeini said:

> If one permits an infidel to continue in his role as a corrupter of the earth, his moral suffering will be all the worse. If one kills the infidel, and thus stops him from perpetrating his misdeeds, his death will be a blessing to him. For if he remains alive, he will become more and more corrupt. This is a surgical operation commanded by God the all-powerful.
>
> . . . [T]hose who follow the teachings of the Koran know that Islam must apply the *lex talionis,* and thus that they must kill. Those who have knowledge of the suffering in the life to come realize that cutting off the hand of someone for a crime he has committed is of benefit to him. In the beyond he will thank those who on earth executed the will of God.
>
> War is a blessing for the world and for all nations. It is God who incites men to fight and to kill. . . . A religion without war is an incomplete religion. If His Holiness Jesus—blessings upon him—had been given more time to live, he would have acted as Moses did and wielded the sword. Those who believe that Jesus did not have "a head for such things," that he was not interested in war, see in him nothing more than a simple preacher, and not a prophet. A prophet is all-powerful. Through war he purifies the earth.
>
> The mullahs with corrupt hearts who say that all this is contrary to the teachings of the Koran are unworthy of Islam. Thanks to God, our young people are now, to the limits of their means, putting God's commandments into action. They know that to kill the unbelievers is one of man's greatest missions.

In many ways, secular religionists, such as the devout and dogmatic rulers in the Soviet Union, Communist China, and in the Palestine Liberation Organization (PLO) are as oppressive of human rights as are the theological and spiritual religionists. For, like the pious transcendentalists, secular religionists also believe in absolutistic thinking, in the sacredness of government, and in the infallibility and holiness of their leaders (Briggs, 1984a, 1984b). They allow for no diversions from their dogmatic structure and condemn anything less than complete sincerity and commitment to their own cause. They reason categorically and ardently support a we-they dichotomy. Those not with them are considered to be against them, and those against them are considered unworthy and punishable. The dogmatic rulers' rigid and irrational demands for absolute patriotism lead them to denigrate, dismiss, and eliminate those whom they deem dissident.

Ironically, enough devout secularists and pious religionists have also been so absolutistic at times that they have violently persecuted transpersonal cults. Note, for example, these interesting items:

Jeremie, Haiti—Thirteen voodoo priests appeared at mass here on a recent Sunday morning and, before the altar of St. Helen's Church, recanted their belief in African spirits and proclaimed their faith in Christianity.

The occasion was tense. A day earlier, lay workers from the Roman Catholic church had smashed the priests' voodoo temples. The parish priest had burned the drums, vessels, potions and crosses that were their cult objects.

Now, by renouncing their "superstitions," the voodoo priests had been told, they could save their lives.

In the three months since the ouster of the Government and the flight of Jean Claude Duvalier to France, where he now lives in a luxury villa inland from the French Riviera, other villagers, many of them from religious groups, have attacked voodoo temples and harassed, threatened and killed their occupants.

According to military, church and local officials, nearly 100 priests and priestesses of Haiti's ancestral religion have been hacked, burned or otherwise put to death by mobs since February. (Simons, 1986 A1, A12)

Tananarive, Madagascar, Aug. 2 (AP)—The Government said today that soldiers backed by armored vehicles had attacked the headquarters of an underground sect based on the martial art of kung fu, killing the sect's leader and 19 of his followers.

An official announcement read over state television said that 31 people were wounded in the attack by Government militiamen on Thursday and that 208 members of the religious sect were arrested.

Reports did not say if the sect members were armed, or if there were any Government casualties in the battle, which was said to have lasted several hours. (Madagascar Kills Twenty in a Sect, *New York Times*, Aug. 3, 1985, 3)

——— • ———

Egypt and Iran persecute followers of the Bahai religion. In many other countries too, God Himself is censored unless He strictly lives up to the local idea of what He ought to be. (Rosenthal, 1988)

Extreme devoutness is evident among the cultists and religionists who, logically following prescribed transpersonal philosophies, denigrate human life on earth in favor of some presumed afterlife and actually encourage their followers literally to kill themselves when faced with adversity. A most dramatic example of this occurred when Jim Jones induced over twelve hundred of his fanatical followers to drink cyanide-laced Kool-Aid in Jonestown, Guyana, in 1978. It was their belief in Jones's "special powers" that predisposed them to comply meekly with his demands.

Another example of the self-destructive capacity of such religious and mystical fanatics is described by Terrence Smith (1984). Smith reports that young boys, aged 12 to 17, were trained by their Iranian leaders to be martyrs in the "holy war" against Iraq. Whipped to a fanatical fervor, they hurled themselves on barbed wire or marched into Iraqi mine fields in the face of withering machine gunfire in order to clear the way for Iranian tanks. "Across the back of their Khaki-colored shirts was stenciled the slogan: 'I have the special permission of the Imam to enter heaven' " (Smith, 1984, p. 21). Similar groups sacrifice their limbs and lives for the causes they deem "holy." Human dependency and need to believe in a higher authority often lead these and other "individuals"(!) to their collective deaths.

John Gross (1987 p. C17), reviewing Amir Taheri's (1987) *Holy Terror: Inside the World of Islam Terrorism,* makes these observations:

> Amir Taheri is an Iranian exile who used to edit the largest daily newspaper in Iran. He has already published a biography of Ayatollah Ruhollah Khomeini; now, in "Holy Terror," he turns his attention to the broader aspects of Islamic terrorism—a phenomenon that will probably still be with us long after Ayatollah Khomeini himself has taken his leave.
>
> Mr. Taheri begins by emphasizing that the Party of God and other Islamic terrorist organizations are religious movements first and last. They are led by religious officials; their ultimate aim is the conversion of the entire world to the faith of Muhammad. This puts them in a quite different class from nationalist movements: the great majority of Yasser Arafat's followers may be Moslems, for example, but it would be misleading to describe the Palestine Liberation Organization itself as "Islamic."
>
> It would also be utterly wrong to equate Islamic terrorism with Islam at large. But this doesn't mean that it can be divorced from its religious roots, any more than the history of the Inquisition (Mr. Taheri's analogy) can be divorced from the history of Christianity. Rather, the terrorists represent one potential form that Islam can take, and a rejection of the other forms that have evolved in the 14 centuries of Islam's existence.

The directly damaging impact that religious and transpersonal cults have on society is evident when one considers the illegal practices of civil disobedience in which many groups engage. Such "organizations" frequently refuse to obey the laws of the communities in which they choose to live in favor of establishing their own governing rules. For example, when asked about his fellow cultists beating their children and refusing to send them to school, one member of the Northeast Kingdom Community Church in Vermont passionately exclaimed: "We are doing this to establish the Kingdom of God on earth. All the best of the world is the Kingdom of Satan" (Butterfield, 1984, p. 16). Such devoutness, rigidity, and a sense of specialness tend to precipitate these groups' refusal to either consider, comply with, or accept the existing social or governing standards. As a result, they may make it unsafe for the rest of us to coexist with so paranoid and fanatical a group.

Numerous "psychotherapy" cults also follow and endorse the transpersonal model and have repeatedly strayed from obeying societal law. Cults such as Synanon and Scientology have had some of their leading members indicted and convicted of stealing, blackmail, breaking into government offices, and other illegal and violent acts. "Thirteen people associated with the Synanon Foundation surrendered in court today to answer charges that they had destroyed evidence about a 1978 attack on a lawyer, using a rattlesnake as a weapon" (Thirteen Synanon Members Answer an Indictment, 1984, p. A21). Other incidents of aggression and violence have also allegedly involved Synanon members. Groups such as these tend to believe that they know the absolute truth and the absolute right and correct ways in which humans must behave. Their leaders serve as all-powerful and unchallenged demigods who brainwash their followers to seek the one and only utopia that they must never leave (Lewin, 1988a). Groups like Synanon operate their own stores, gas stations, and other businesses and make fortunes from their mindless, passive, unchallenging, and devout members.

Another example of the dangers associated with devout and fanatical groups is evident in the increasingly popular devil-worshipping cults (Laurence, 1974; LaVey, 1972). Many of these cults and groups are inspired by the works of Carlos Castaneda (1968, 1984) and other aficionados of transpersonal psychology. Satanic cultists, like the group in Northport, New York, whose members ritually killed a seventeen-year-old boy and burned and tortured animals in satanic rituals (McFadden, 1984), keep springing up in different regions of the United States and abroad. There has also been an apparent increase in satanically oriented lyrics in rock-and-roll music, with which today's adolescent record buyers sometimes identify. Satanic symbols are often worn on articles of clothing and used in acts of vandalism. Although teenagers may deny endorsement of satanic principles, many will still purchase satanic bibles and a number wear satanic T-shirts, jewelry, and other articles to be in vogue. The influence of such cults has begun to reach greater and more disconcerting proportions.

Terrorism, inspired by religious and mystical creeds and by extreme nationalism (which itself is one of the main forms of devout religiosity), has been widespread in recent years and shows no signs of waning. According to Colby (1984, p. 15), terrorism is "a tactic of indiscriminate violence used against innocent bystanders for political effect." Most terroristic attacks, moreover, are the result of fanatical and blind allegiance to a religious or nationalistic cause. We contend that this kind of ideology is often created and promulgated by passionate mystical beliefs.

The specialness or entitlement that fanatical groups often attribute to themselves is pervasive and enduring. This is most evident in those religious and transpersonal cults that endorse the Armageddon prophecy and preach that it will soon arrive. They assert that "only those who accept the Lord, Jesus Christ, will be saved. All the others—those who worship in the name of other religions or who embrace no religion—are doomed to everlasting punishments and torture" (Negri, 1984, p. 27). Such grandiosity often leads organized groups such as the Jehovah's Witnesses to proselytize their version of the Bible and dismiss others' perspectives as "uniformed" and "wrong." Categorical thinking, as such, facilitates and maintains prejudice, bigotry, and bias and often ultimately leads many groups to organized acts of aggression.

Orthodox and fundamentalist Christian and Islamic sects are, of course, not the only religious groups that resort to violence. Thus, in commenting on the devout Judaism of Meir Kahane, Smerling (1985, p. A35) notes that "Kahanism blends ultra nationalism with fundamentalism, racism and legitimatized violence. It casts aside democratic values in pursuit of its higher goals." Confirming this, Kahane (1985, p. A35) states: "Jews must choose Judaism and Zionism over Western democracy."

Religion, again, often has some excellent antiracist, antinationalistic, and democratic aspects. But devout religiosity (Ellis, 1983b) is quite another matter! Similarly, absolutistic and authoritarian transpersonalism tends, by its very dogmatic nature, to take on violent accoutrements. Not always, but often enough!

In our own century, we have recently had many terrorist acts committed by devout religionists against birth control and abortion clinics. Thus, a former Benedictine monk, Joe Scheidler of the Pro-Life Action League, said of the bombers of such clinics: "Maybe they're right in bombing the clinics. I don't know. God told the Israelites, when they went to Canaan, to destroy all the temples, the priests, the pagans and the people who were doing perverted things" (Anti-Abortion Activitist Says Clinic Bombers May Be Right, 1985).

Samuel G. Freedman (1987, pp. B1, B4) paints a picture of an abortion bombing suspect, Dennis John Malvasi, and shows how he was influenced by a Catholic cult:

> In his furtive new life, Mr. Malvasi received telephone calls by beeper, collected his mail at several bars and "lived out of a sea bag." One of the friends who put him up from time to time was Edmund H. Janiszewski, a Vietnam combat veteran with a full disability for mental stress that he says was caused by wartime exposure to toxic herbicides.
>
> While most friends did not know of Mr. Malvasi's strong and conservative Catholicism, Mr. Janiszewski shared it. He also introduced Mr. Malvasi to Our Lady of the Roses, a renegade movement led by Veronica Lueken, a Long Island housewife who claims that the Virgin Mary and Jesus Christ appear to and speak through her.
>
> The Catholic Diocese of Brooklyn has investigated her claims, declared them groundless, and denounced the movement. Nonetheless, Mrs. Lueken has an estimated 60,000 followers in North America. They

apparently respond to her contentions that, for instance, Satan attended the Second Vatican Council and Pope Paul VI was kidnapped, drugged and replaced by an imposter for the last six years of his reign.

And abortion, Mrs. Lueken has frequently said, is "the foulest of sacrileges." In May 1986, she told a crowd that Jesus was saying to her: "We cannot tolerate the murders of the unborn. This is a sacrilege of the most foul manner in the eyes of the Eternal Father, and shall be punishable by death."

It would take a thick volume all its own to discuss in detail the instances of terrorism, including the maiming and murdering of innocent citizens of many different countries, that have recently occurred. So let us mention only a few that seem to have been clearly instigated by terrorist individuals or groups who are absolutely sure that they know the Right (religious, mystical, nationalistic, or racist) Way and that all "infidels" who do not follow this Way are totally undeserving of life, liberty, or the pursuit of happiness.

Some of the recent terrorist outrages perpetrated by fanatical religions and mystical groups include these:

Paris, Sept. 17—A bomb that the authorities said had been thrown from a passing car exploded in front of a crowded department store on the Left Bank today, killing at least 5 people and wounding about 50.

It was the most lethal of five terrorist attacks to shake this city in the last 10 days.

The bombing deepened an already acute sense of insecurity in the French capital, where many people are already curbing their activities and avoiding crowded places. It occurred, despite a general mobilization of security forces and an intensive police hunt for those responsible for the terror campaign, which is believed to be aimed at freeing Arab guerrillas jailed in France. (Bernstein, 1986, A1, A11)

Istanbul, Turkey, Sept. 6—The Arab terrorists invaded a Sephardic synagogue during Sabbath services in the Jewish quarter here today and, after locking the doors with iron bars, attacked the congregation with submachine guns and hand grenades.

At least 21 worshippers, including rabbis, were killed, and 4 others were wounded in the massacre, a blaze of gunfire and explosions that went on for three to five minutes and left the newly refurbished synagogue on fire. The bodies of both gunmen were found in the carnage.

Witnesses described scenes of horror as bullets from automatic weapons raked the benches, worshippers in prayer shawls screamed and fell and blasts shook the Neve Shalom Synagogue, the city's largest, in the Karakoy district near the Galata Tower. One report said the killers also poured gasoline on some victims and tried to burn the bodies.

A "Horrifying" Scene

"It's horrifying," Hasan All Ozer, Istanbul's Deputy Governor, said after visiting the scene. Interior Minister Yildirim Akbulut said the killers had barred the synagogue's main doors to keep people from escaping the bullets and grenades. Only 4 of the 29 worshippers escaped unhurt. (Kamm, 1985, A1)

———— • ————

Rome, Dec. 27—Terrorists hurled grenades and fired submachine guns at crowds of holiday travelers at airports in Rome and Vienna today in attacks on check-in counters of El Al Israel Airlines.

Authorities quoted by news services said the gunmen had killed at least 13 people, including 4 Americans, and wounded 113 in the two attacks. Four terrorists were killed, and three others were wounded and captured.

While El Al appeared to be a target in both attacks, the authorities said the terrorists in Rome had also thrown grenades and fired indiscriminately with Soviet-made assault rifles into crowds of New York–bound passengers checking in at Pan American World Airways and Trans World Airlines. (Tagliabue, 1985, 1, 4)

Jerusalem, Dec. 29—Defense Minister Yitzhak Rabin said today that it was Israel's initial assessment that the shadowy, pro-Libyan Palestinian terrorist group Abu Nidal was responsible for the Rome and Vienna airport attacks.

"I cannot say for sure," Mr. Rabin told a visiting American delegation, "but that is our impression."

In Rome the head of Italian military intelligence said that the four terrorists who killed 12 people there Friday were members of the Abu Nidal group and that they had been trained in Iran. The Ministry of Defense distanced itself from the official's remarks but diplomats in Rome and British and other Italian intelligence aides lent weight to the contention that Iran may have been involved. (Friedman, 1985, A1, A8)

——— • ———

If this is the decade of the terrorist, then 1985 was one of its highlights. The hijackings of two planes and a cruise ship, and new outbreaks of terrorist frenzy in the Middle East and Western Europe mark the desperate truth of Lenin's words: "The purpose of terrorism is to terrorize." And the purpose of terrorizing is to weaken the will of the terrorist's opponent. (Roelofsma, 1986, 59)

——— • ———

Beirut, Lebanon, June 21—Hundreds of Moslem demonstrators chanting "Death to America" and "Death to Reagan" held a mass rally at the international airport here today, where they cheered the hijackers of the T.W.A. airliner.

The march was organized by the pro-Iranian Shiite group called the Party of God, whose members were believed to have commandeered the Boeing 727 last Friday.

In some ways, it was a scene reminiscent of the Iranian hostage crisis that ended in 1981. Many of the demonstrators carried huge posters of Iran's fundamentalist Shiite leader, Ayatollah Ruhollah Khomeini. (Hijazi, 1985)

London, June 23—An Air-India Boeing 747 plunged into the sea off the Irish coast today, apparently killing all 329 people on board, and an Indian official said an explosion was believed to have caused the crash.

Ashok Ghelok, the Minister of State for Civil Aviation, said in New Delhi that there was "a distinct possibility" the plane had been destroyed by a bomb. He said an explosion of some sort was "considered to be the cause" of the disaster. (Apple, Jr., 1985, A1)

——— • ———

Amman, Jordan—Bombings are virtually a normal occurrence in Beirut—there had been one in the same neighborhood about a week before—but even by local standards, the explosion on March 8, the Moslem Sabbath, was massive. At least 80 people were killed and 200 wounded in the densely populated Shiite neighborhood. The explosion went off on the doorstep of Sheikh Mohammed Hussein Fadallah, the fiery preacher who is widely believed to be the inspiration behind the rapidly growing fundamentalist Party of God movement. Several of his bodyguards were killed, but he was untouched; he had stopped to speak with an elderly woman follower, varying his routine by minutes.

Much of the new terrorism is believed to be abetted from Iran, where a kind of Shiite International is in touch with local agents who propagate Ayatollah Ruhollah Khomeini's Islamic revolution. Iran has supported a Shiite group in Iraq known as Al Dawa. Iraqi and Lebanese members of Al Dawa were sentenced to death in Kuwait for their part in the bombings, which damaged the American and French Embassies. (Kiffner, 1985a, B5)

——— • ———

Istanbul, Turkey, Nov. 13—A draft report prepared for lawmakers from the 16-member Atlantic alliance concludes that international terrorism is becoming more sophisticated, increasingly sponsored by Middle Eastern countries, and deadlier each year.

The 52-page report singles out Syria, Iran, and Libya as countries that have "actively" sponsored international terrorism, along with the Palestine Liberation Organization. It says the P.L.O. is a "government in waiting" whose diplomatic missions and large fund-raising operations have supported terrorist actions

The report concludes that although bombings and assassinations will continue as the "preferred" weapons of terrorists in the foreseeable future, "there is a danger that terrorists will begin to employ more sophisticated means of sabotage, such as either damaging high-technology computer networks or poisoning water, food supplies, or household products," as terrorist groups become more sophisticated. (J. Miller, 1986, 51)

Of all the differences between rational-emotive therapy and transpersonal psychology, their differences regarding anger, damnation, and violence are probably the most salient and most important. For although the irreparable conflicts between opposing devout religious ideologies, political groups, and cultist factions have done immense harm in the past, the state of weaponry then allowed the human race to survive. In spite of all the killings, wars, and genocide to which such conflicts often led, there existed little threat to the overall existence of humankind. For when humans used knives and bows and arrows, and even when they used guns and bombs to "solve" their interpersonal or interideological conflicts, they were able to slaughter each other by the millions and still survive. In today's nuclear age, of course, the threat is literally earth-shattering.

According to many leading authorities (Schell, 1982, 1984), nuclear war could easily lead to the extermination of the planet and the entire human race. As Raloff (1984) illustrates, other deadly weapons such as lasers and particle beams are now being developed that could also lead to a level of slaughter undreamed of in the past. With the ever-increasing, widespread, and irreparable damage that can be wreaked by modern weaponry, for the continued existence of humankind, we must do our best to hold in check paranoid and fanatical individuals and groups who believe that by slaughtering the world they are saving it.

As noted, the advent and accessibility of nuclear weaponry could ultimately lead to the destruction of humankind if placed in the hands of fanatical, paranoid, and self-entitled mystical and religious groups (Ellis, 1983b, 1986a). Many philosophers, psychologists, and dignitaries have agreed with this view. As Paul Warnke (1984, p. 8) writes, "A tyrant or religious zealot could, for a time, make himself king of the hill." (Or, we might add, make herself queen of the hill.) Although this concern is shared by increasing numbers of people, many educated individuals do not see the degree or extent of the danger and threat from transpersonal oriented fanatics.

Let us by all means stress the increasing dangers that are likely to result from endorsement of a transpersonal philosophy. Mystical, religious, and political zealots all over the world already resort to innumerable acts of terrorism with conventional weapons. As a result of advancing technology, it is likely, and unfortunately, only a matter of time before a small group of such fanatics can manufacture nuclear or other deadly weapons in their basements or churches. When this time arrives—probably within the next hundred years or so—such fanatical and transpersonally oriented groups, righteously and fervently believing that they know the one and only Secret Doctrine and Universal Truth, and devoutly holding that their members will be deified and rise to heaven while the rest of us false believers will be devil-ified and sink to hell when the end of the world comes, will be very likely to push the nuclear or other buttons deliberately and send most or all of us to eternity (Ellis, 1983b, 1986a; Hamburg, 1986).

If our concerns about the potential threat to humankind are realistic—and we truly hope that they are not—then fanatical mysticism and religiosity had better be checked by rational-emotive therapy and other effective, scientifically oriented forms of psychological education. Otherwise, we or our descendants face the likelihood of transpersonal fanatics destroying themselves to meet their Makers, and taking the rest of us with them. This is a serious problem for the human race in general, and for psychotherapeutic education in particular!

Let us conclude this chapter on the hostility, damnation, and terrorism inspired by devout religious and transpersonal dogmas with a quotation from John R. Baker (1986, p. 34):

Harm develops when a small group of intolerant believers manages to gain sufficient adherents to achieve political power. This leads to censorship, persecution, and a retreat of civilization. Harm also results when so many persons hold mystical beliefs that only simplistic thinking is applied to complex problems. Even in this century, the chaos resulting from simplistic thinking and intolerance could lead to a new dark age.

9

Discouraging the Acceptance of Uncertainty and Probability

In order to reduce human neuroses, most schools of psychotherapy seek to help people increase their acceptance of life's probabilities and uncertainties. Thus, clients learn to accept that life is not, or need not be, totally predictable or "knowable." They learn to accept life's natural ambiguities and even the tentativeness of their own existence. Clients experience minimal anxiety by surrendering their demands for certitude. They abandon their "need" for guarantees in a life full of inexactitude. They thereby reduce their depression, rage, and horror.

Rational-emotive therapy holds that, as far as is known, there are no absolute certainties in the world (Ellis, 1973a, 1983b, 1988). On the contrary, RET views life through more realistic and objective lenses and sees it, instead, as replete with uncertainty. It is, therefore, only with high (or low) degrees of probability, and not with 100 percent assurance, that various things can be known or accomplished.

Despite the omnipresence of uncertainty, indeterminacy, and dubiosity, people, especially those with fanatical or mystical penchants, demand that they must have Absolute Knowledge and, contrary to a lack of supporting evidence, assert that it is, in fact, obtainable. Such individuals believe that they *need* complete certainty and that they especially need certain or absolute "meaning" in their lives. They refuse to accept that, as far as one can empirically, logically, or realistically determine, there is *no* cosmic or sacrosanct meaning. Yet, people continue dogmatically to embrace their unrealistic demands for certitude (Ellis, 1962, 1973a, 1983b, 1987b, 1987d, 1988). Rational-emotive therapy helps them to become secure by accepting insecurity and ambiguity and by giving up their irrational demands for total meaning and certainty.

While RET asserts that it is not only unrealistic but also dysfunctional to demand or command anything from life, transpersonal psychology insists that it is actually good for people to have incontrovertible faith and dogmatic conviction in unchangeable absolutes. To prove that certainty is attainable, and since they believe that it is functional to "know" it, transpersonal devotees often blindly convince themselves that, despite nonexistent and disconfirming data, phenomena such as ESP, ghosts, fortune-telling, psychic surgery, elves, fairies, goblins, astrology, voodoo, and other paranormal experiences exist (Agena, 1983; All Together, Now: Meditate, 1985; Asimov, 1984; Fichten, 1984; Gardner, 1986; Hansel, 1984; Harper, 1983, Kurtz, 1985a, 1986a). (Also see the evidence that we present in chapter 5.)

Transpersonalists' dogmatic demand for certainty is also evident in many of their case scenarios. Consider a case cited by Fritz (1984). Desperate for certainty, two pregnant women at Fritz's workshop on creating the ideal birth stoutly claimed to have had telepathic contact with their unborn children. Most of the other workshop participants believed them!

The preponderance of the transpersonalists' need for certainty is also evident in more common, everyday examples. Witness, alas, the many astrologists, fortune-tellers, and tarot-card readers that one can find by merely thumbing through the *Yellow Pages*. Since advertising in the *Yellow Pages* and in local town newspapers is expensive, we may assume that these "sages" are making enough money to cover their carrying costs. This illustrates the demand for such services in our American population. If Nancy and Ronald Reagan take these seers seriously enough to let them influence political decisions (Regan, 1988), why should not all the rest of us indulge in this kind of certainty seeking?

Typically, "seers" seem to make reasonable incomes from ostensibly reading the futures of their clientele. Unbeknown to these clients, however, soothsayers typically offer them "Barnum" statements that can apply to anyone. These general statements are similar to those seen in newspaper horoscope columns. However, the naive believer sees that they "clearly" predict his or her personal life and, therefore, concludes that they are "indubitably" valid and accurate.

Other "evidence" used to support the "validity" of fortune-telling is that the predicted future sometimes actually comes true. While general predictions may often prove accurate for just about anyone (since they are in fact *general*), some others are realized by means of self-fulfilling prophesies. By merely believing that something will come true, we may unconsciously and inadvertently make it come true. As a result, fortune-tellers make a great deal of money by exploiting people's irrational beliefs that they *must* know their fates and that the uncertainty of *not* knowing is unbearable. Rather than helping their devotees to modify or restructure such irrationalities, many transpersonalists reinforce these fallacious notions of needing certainty to secure their own personal gains.

Individuals who demand intellectual certainty also tend to demand emotional certainty or the guarantee that they will always be in total control of their feelings. They avoid losing complete emotional control by using distraction strategies, such as compulsively reciting a mantra or by denying that they feel anxiety. Rather than teaching their clients how to minimize their self-defeating emotional reactions, transpersonal psychotherapists encourage emotional "control" that turns off emotions. As a result, clients fail to experience appropriate emotional highs and lows and, instead, often strive to feel "calmness" or "nothing." Please remember that *Nirvana* does not mean *bliss* (as many Americans wrongly believe) but *desirelessness*. And who can be happy in *that* state?!

Although some devout religionists, mystics, and true believers can superficially "let go" and "be themselves" (Ellis, 1972c), many of them believe that they must always have thorough control over themselves and the universe. They feel terrorized by any potential emotional looseness, opting for extreme stoic, asocial, and flat existences. They will not allow themselves to feel and express emotions freely and spontaneously because they cannot be absolutely sure of the outcome of these experiences. They often believe that they must always be completely controlled. Rational-emotive therapy, on the other hand, not only helps people minimize their emotional disturbances, but also helps them to become more emotionally alive. By encouraging people to develop vital and absorbing interests, as will be discussed later, it encourages them to achieve emotional heights, rather than extremes of disturbing affect or no affect (Ellis, 1985, 1988; Ellis & Becker, 1982).

Whereas RET helps clients accept an uncertain and often unpredictable world, transpersonal psychologists deny that the world is actually an uncertain place and that accepting this is valuable. Rather, they argue that certainty can be known and that such absolute knowledge is attainable through paranormal means. Rational-emotive therapists encourage clients to perceive, interpret, and evaluate the world logically and empirically. Transpersonalists abjure this kind of realism and practicality (Barron, 1987; Bhatty, 1987; Bufe, 1987; Ehrlich, 1986; Kinzer, 1987; Gusic, 1988).

Ironically, when transpersonalists accept uncertainty and probability, they try to prove that *anything* goes and that therefore mysticism is "true" and "valid" (Capra, 1983; Ferguson, 1980). As Wilczek and Devine (1988) indicate, linking Taoist mysticism and parapsychological mumbo-jumbo "is a pernicious idea, which has led many good minds wildly astray." Restivo (1983) also attacks Capra's (1983) claims that there are parallels between modern physics and ancient mysticism.

10

Discouraging Personal Choice and Will

Most major schools of psychotherapy emphasize some degree of free will and personal choice, though the idea of complete determinism has been practically abandoned in modern psychology. Although biological and genetic limits on human potential and personality exist, people are not necessarily totally governed by their physiology and are not programmed to be just one way or have one set destiny. Their lives, instead, are biased by both their genetic markers and environmental conditioning (Ellis, 1976a). They do, however, have some flexibility or choice of how they think, feel, and act (Ellis, 1962, 1972a, 1973a, 1977f, 1988).

Rational-emotive therapy holds that humans are limited by their biological natures and does not endorse the naive view of J. B. Watson (1919) that they are solely the product of their environments and learning histories. Such a view ignores research in genetics and the interaction between nature and nurture. Therefore, RET acknowledges this interaction and stresses that people had better work to change themselves and their disturbances as much as their biological tendencies will allow. For example, if people are limited by a biochemical brain disorder, such as mental deficiency or schizophrenia, that limits their potential for achieving high degrees of productivity and happiness, they *can* still work to maximize the extent to which they *are* capable of such achievements. Rational-emotive therapy, therefore, endorses a much more optimistic and humanistic stance than the more deterministically based schools of psychotherapy.

Rational-emotive therapy contends that humans have strong innate tendencies to think about their thinking and to be able to decide their own emotional destinies (Ellis, 1962, 1973a, 1984a, 1984b, 1987a, 1988; Ellis & Harper, 1975). Although it holds that humans do not have perfect free will, they are somewhat (not totally) able to change their thinking and to modify their emotional and behavioral responses to their environments. People *do* have some "will" and *can* exercise their options to change their thinking, their emoting, and their behaving.

Whereas the less cognitively oriented schools of psychotherapy consider past events or environmental stimuli primarily responsible for human neuroses, rational-emotive therapy tries to help clients accept responsibility for their part in making themselves disturbed and for strongly choosing to work at changing themselves. Because RET emphasizes the importance of cognition in human disturbance, clients learn to modify their thinking in more rational and realistic directions to minimize their self-defeating distresses and maximize their long-term productivity.

Transpersonal psychology differs from rational-emotive therapy in that although it sometimes favors will, personal choice, and self-change, it also frequently holds that we are ruled by inexorable karma or fate. Transpersonalists typically argue that even our thinking and our choices to change our behavior are fatalistically predetermined. This is another example of the transpersonal penchant for creating unfalsifiable hypotheses and dogmatically stating that these hypotheses are "known" to be undeniable facts.

The transpersonal position with respect to free will and personal choice is, therefore, highly equivocal and contradictory. Transpersonalists often assert that humans really cannot control or manage their own physical and mental destinies (Bhatty, 1983; Rama, 1982). Yet, they also teach their followers to turn off their emotional excesses so as to achieve "non-feeling" states. They apparently believe that such a choice is really not chosen! Transpersonalists, therefore, frequently include a deterministic philosophy that is pessimistic and that advocates helplessness.

Transpersonal psychology also differs from RET in that it tends to be ultraconservative and displays rigid allegiance to tradition and to the past (Levine, 1984; Neese, 1984). Rational-emotive therapy avers that because people are innately impressionable or gullible, their early experiences influence their goals and standards but have much less impact on their rigid and disturbed efforts to create absolute musts *about* these roles. Moreover, although life experiences may contribute to the development of people's personal beliefs or life philosophy, their persistent choosing, in the here-and-now, to *continue* to endorse and hold on to these beliefs primarily leads to their cognitive-emotive-behavioral disturbances. Rational-emotive therapy does not dismiss the past as irrelevant in contributing to personality or attitude development. It maintains that, for effective therapy, people had better focus on their current decisions to continue thinking crookedly and behaving inappropriately. As stated previously, the rational-emotive philosophy and approach is, therefore, significantly more optimistic than the transpersonal approach. It shows people how their current endorsement of irrational beliefs now serves to maintain their level of disturbances and how they can choose, in the here-and-now, to change their thinking and reduce their disturbances (Bard, 1987, 1988; Ellis, 1962, 1971, 1973a, 1977a, 1979c, 1981a, 1985, 1988; Ellis & Abrahms, 1978; Ellis & Harper, 1975; Grieger & Boyd, 1980; Grieger & Grieger, 1982; Walen, DiGiuseppe & Wessler, 1980; Wessler & Wessler, 1980).

The acceptance of one's limitations and innate human fallibility is a goal common to most therapeutic modalities. Acceptance of human fallibility leads to self-acceptance, which is achieved when people accept themselves and others unconditionally, *whether or not* they fail and *whether or not* significant others approve of them (Ellis, 1962, 1972b, 1973a, 1976c, 1985, 1988; Ellis & Dryden, 1987; Ellis & Harper, 1975; Lazarus, 1977).

Rational-emotive therapy teaches that all humans are exceptionally fallible by nature, and that realistically we had better expect them to err often and commit many undesirable acts. As we are not perfect in our biological, psychological, and emotional makeups, we may expect numerous flaws, limitations, sins, misdeeds, and blunders. Even Christian philosophy asserts that humans are not perfect and are yet forgivable.

Rational-emotive therapy, like some parts of Christian philosophy, teaches people to accept themselves and others fully *with* their fallibility. It shows them how to make the best of their imperfections. It encourages them not to denigrate themselves for their limitations (Ellis, 1962, 1973a, 1977a, 1988; Hauck, 1973, 1979) and to increase their tolerance of others. Thereby they can maximize individual happiness and social cooperation (Ellis, 1988; Ellis & Becker, 1982).

Many transpersonally oriented groups are demanding and intractable about human fallibility. Many devout political factions and religious sects are as intolerant of the flaws and mistakes of their own members as they are of the attitudes and policies of people in other organizations that hold different credos. Such intolerance is often at the core of both religious and political wars, as we noted in chapter 8. Transpersonalists harbor absolutistic and unyielding notions about the ways that they themselves and others must think and behave; they are not only irrational but also dangerous to society.

Transpersonal psychology is often quite perfectionistic about the human condition. Many sects refer to the God within each individual and tell clients that "you are perfect the way you are" and that you *must* remain perfect. Transpersonal psychology frequently insists that people can be godlike and virtually eliminate all human ills and failings by accepting Absolute Truth (Amritu, 1982; Bhatty, 1984a; E. Brown, 1984; Fairfield, 1984; Ferguson, 1980; Stace, 1960; Rosicrucians, 1984). This demand for perfection leads not only to anxiety, depression, shame, and guilt when personal failure occurs, but also to anger, damnation, intolerance, and aggression when other people fail.

The dire need for perfection often fosters grandiosity. For example, a number of fundamentalist and transpersonal sects believe that only they know God's truths or the "secret of it all," and that the rest of us mere mortals will remain forever ignorant. They assert that, come Judgment Day, those without this "bounty" will be severely punished (Butterfield, 1984; Frick, 1982; Starr, 1984). What an extraordinary sense of entitlement!

Perfection is an almost undefinable and sometimes contradictory concept. Thus, some transcendentalists consider a human to be "perfect" but also see his or her traits as changeable for the "better." If so, how could he or she be "perfect" to begin with? Yet, despite the illogic of such a concept, transpersonal factions commonly endorsed it.

The goal of RET is to help people accept that they are, and most probably always will be, fallible, "sinning," and error making. It never encourages rational emotivists to become apathetic or unconcerned about their sins or limitations but actively helps them to remedy their failings so as to maximize their productivity and happiness. Rational-emotive therapy helps people accept the rational belief that just because they *do* bad things, *feel* bad emotionally, or *think* bad thoughts, this does not make them "bad *people*."

To assume that one can and must become perfect is not only irrational, but also iatrogenic. It predisposes people to be dysfunctional in several ways, some of which we have already addressed. In addition to producing needless turmoil, increased lack of cooperation, and distancing from others, people who believe that they *need* to be perfect tend to be distraught about their current performances and status. The need for perfection, therefore, discourages them from enjoying themselves or their state of affairs in the here-and-now. It tends to bar them from seeing and learning from their mistakes and to push them to berate themselves globally for their inadequacies.

Transpersonal psychology often encourages "radical trans-formation." As Charlene Szymusiak (1985, p. 38) notes, "Radical transformation isn't just being adjusted or having a spiritual high. It reasons that, within a *few years* of doing this practice, you will open your eyes and gaze upon your original perfection. It reasons that your day-to-day conduct—how you relate to other human beings, temptations, and pressures—will begin to reflect that perfection. That's radical change."

Similar perfectionistic notions have been espoused by many other transpersonal leaders and groups (Bordewich, 1988; Ehrlich, 1986; Goleman, 1979; Hock, 1983; Lindsey, 1987; Morain, 1988; Schneider, 1987). The almost inevitable result? Much ultimate disillusionment and anguish!

11

Blocking Insight and Awareness

Insight and awareness are concepts addressed by all major schools of psychotherapy, though divergent schools define them differently. We can view insight as understanding the original (or early) causes and/or as discerning the current causes of disorders. Insight may also include "getting in touch with one's feelings" or coming up with a problem-solving answer to difficulties. In terms of these concepts, rational-emotive therapy and transpersonal psychotherapy tend to differ significantly.

Transpersonal psychologists tend to espouse mystical, all-encompassing, and transcendental "insight." They often claim that the gaining of "higher consciousness," "heightened awareness," and "unified" insight will by itself produce miraculous personality changes (Capra, 1983; Deikman, 1972; Maharishi Mahesh Yogi, 1983; Mann, 1984; Shah, 1982; Tulku, 1977, 1978). This view is hardly that of RET!

Rational-emotive therapy emphasizes three types of insight that are important for clients to accept in order to facilitate personality change. These insights are more realistic, pragmatic, and concrete than those sought by transpersonal psychologists.

Rational-emotive therapy contends that it is important for people to realize, first, that they, themselves, largely create their own emotional disturbance by accepting or inventing absolutistic demands for themselves, for others, and for their environment. It asserts that individuals had better work to identify the unconditional shoulds and musts that they endorse and that help make them disturbed. The first type of RET insight, therefore, is to help people see and agree that, in RET terminology, A (an Activating Event) does not produce C (an emotional or behavioral Consequence). Rather, B (people's Belief system) creates C. Thus, sticks and stones may break your bones and directly cause you physical pain, but names, words, deeds, and other Activating Events do not hurt you *emotionally*. Your emotional pains are, instead, a function of the ways you perceive, interpret, and evaluate interpersonal and world conditions.

The second insight RET clients are encouraged to accept is that no matter how or where or when they originally made themselves disturbed, they now, in the present, are continuing to upset themselves. If the client's emotional upset stems directly from events that occurred in the past, since he/she cannot have them *un*occur, the client will *always* have to be disturbed. Yet, as experience shows, clients can get over past, unchangeable events. They undo the influence of these events because clients modify the ways they think, feel, and act about past occurrences. RET shows them how to discern what they *continue* to think and how they *maintain* their old disturbances.

The third insight or realization that RET encourages people to recognize is that there is no magical or passive way to eliminate or minimize their disturbances. Rather, they need to resort to *steady and consistent work and practice. Knowledge* of irrational beliefs and the acceptance of some degree of responsibility for individual disturbance will likely help the client. But only through his/her diligent *efforts* at restructuring beliefs, feelings, and behaviors is the client likely to achieve personality modification. Awareness and insight, in and of themselves, will be helpful; but *hard work* at *applying* RET's insights No. 1 and No. 2 is most important!

Let us consider the notion that insight alone can lead to desired therapeutic changes. Consider, for example, that a couple enters psychotherapy to correct a problem of low sex desire. What are their individual goals? Each can ask himself and his partner this very question. Do they want therapy merely to help themselves understand *why* they have this problem? Or, do they also want it to help themselves *get over* it? Obviously, the preference is toward the latter solution.

Too often, people believe that merely by knowing or having insight into the source(s) of their problems they will remove them. How unlikely! A person's mere knowledge that he/she became sexually uninterested because of an ultraconservative upbringing or because of being damned every time a sexual thought emerged will not automatically lead to sexual spontaneity. A more direct approach is needed to *change* thinking and behaving. The client may find it interesting to go back later and try to determine what caused his/her problems, but that knowledge alone (if it is found) will seldom solve anything. Also, people who get over their problems are rarely concerned with why they got them in the first place. Viable therapeutic solutions, therefore, require direct interventions beyond a mere understanding of how a client came to be the way he/she is.

Rational-emotive therapy and transpersonal psychotherapy dramatically differ with respect to their utilization and understanding of insight and awareness. Whereas the transpersonal perspective is bent toward more metaphysical and abstract notions of disturbance and is unlikely to lead to nondisturbance, RET stresses practical insights (Ellis, 1962, 1971, 1973a, 1988; Ellis & Dryden, 1987; Ellis & Harper, 1975). As a result, RET is more active, directive, and effort oriented than its transpersonal counterpart.

As will be shown in chapter 15, RET is much more integrative and systemic than is TP (Ellis, 1984e, 1985, 1987a, 1987e, 1988, 1989; Ellis and Dryden, 1987). Even in the area of cognition, it not only uses several kinds of insight, such as those described at the beginning of this chapter, but it also makes use of several other cognitive methods that transpersonal therapy ignores. These include:

1. *Referenting.* When people refuse to give up their harmful behaviors (such as procrastination or smoking) and when they push out of mind the disadvantages of their addictions, RET encourages them to make a list of all the self-defeating results of their compulsions and a list of the advantages of stopping them. They then reread and actively think about these lists several times a day to help themselves surrender their addictions and compulsions.

2. *Reframing.* Clients who seriously panic and depress themselves about the unfortunate events in their lives (such as failures and rejections) are shown how to focus on the *good* aspects of these bad things. Thus, if you get rejected by a potential sex or love partner, you can show yourself how beneficial it is that you quickly discovered that this person is not for you, and thereby saved yourself much wasted time and energy by not continuing to pursue this person.

   Rational-emotive therapy particularly shows people how to reframe their dysfunctional feelings and behaviors so that instead of horrifying themselves about them, they accept the challenge of dealing with them, changing them, and refusing to denigrate themselves for having them (Ellis, 1988).

3. *Cognitive distraction.* Rational-emotive therapy tries to help people change their disordered feelings by uprooting the philosophic sources of these disorders. It also palliatively uses various forms of cognitive distraction (such as thought stopping, progressive relaxation, and entertainment) to help people calm themselves down so that they can *then* employ more elegant disputing techniques. Unlike other forms of therapy (including TP), RET *first* employs cognitive distraction techniques but *also* goes on to more permanent disputing of people's irrational beliefs.

4. *Modeling.* As Bandura (1977) has shown, modeling is an effective mode of cognitive therapy. Whereas transpersonal ther-

apists often model disturbed behavior (such as shamanistic rituals and trance states), RET practitioners model more rational and productive behaviors (such as undisturbedly accepting and coping with unfortunate events and problems).

5. *Uprooting secondary disturbances.* Rational-emotive therapy assumes that people often have both primary *and* secondary emotional disturbances. When they tell themselves, "I *must* not fail!" and "I *have to* be approved by others!" they first make themselves anxious and/or depressed. Then, noting that they feel upset, they frequently tell themselves, "I *must* not be anxious!" or *"I can't stand* being depressed!" and then make themselves panicked about their panic or depressed about their depression. Rational-emotive therapy therefore first shows them how to surrender their secondary disturbances (by accepting themselves *with* their primary feelings of anxiety and depression) and then deals with their primary disturbances and shows them how to think, feel, and act in order to dispel them.

6. *Coping statements.* Rational-emotive therapy shows people how to dispute their irrational beliefs (at point B in the ABCDEs of rational-emotive therapy), but it also shows them how to create and steadily employ (at point E, Effective New Philosophy) rational coping statements. Thus, clients and others who use RET write down and often repeat to themselves—and *think* through, instead of merely suggestively parroting—self-statements like "I do not *need* what I want. I *prefer* it but can also live happily without it." "I would very much *like* people to treat me fairly and considerately, but they never *have to*!" "A *hassle* is not a *horror*. It is highly inconvenient for me to be rejected, but it's not the end of the world!"

7. *Imagery and visualization.* Where transpersonalists often use unrealistic and pollyannaish positive imagery (such as visualizing one's "good" body cells devouring one's "bad"

cancerous cells), RET uses practical imagery and behavioral rehearsal (such as visualizing oneself playing tennis satisfactorily or speaking well in public) to help people have increased confidence in their performances. It also uses rational-emotive imagery, as explained in chapter 15.

8. *Psychoeducational methods.* Rational-emotive therapy does not merely rely on individual and group therapy sessions to help people overcome their problems. With clients and members of the public, RET also uses many psychoeducational techniques such as pamphlets, books, charts, graphs, talks, courses, audio and video cassettes, films, workshops, marathons, and intensives. These educational resources can speed and intensify individual and group therapy and significantly help many individuals who never come for therapy. Thus, the regular Friday-night "Problems in Everyday Living" workshop that I (A.E.) give at the Institute for Rational-Emotive Therapy in New York City has, over the last quarter of a century, helped tens of thousands of people. Through experiencing me talking to volunteers about their personal problems, people in the audience can see that they themselves have emotional difficulties and can deal with them by using the same techniques that I demonstrate to the volunteers.

9. *Recording of sessions.* Rational-emotive therapy clients are encouraged to record their own therapy sessions and listen to them one or more times, to hear various points that they may have missed during the live sessions. Clients frequently report that they get as much or more from listening to the recordings as they get from the original sessions.

10. *Problem solving.* As RET practitioners help their clients to see that their rational and irrational beliefs create in them appropriate and inappropriate feelings, they also encourage clients to replace their Jehovian demands and commands with

their wishes and preferences. In addition, RET therapists help these clients to reconsider their practical problems and to figure out better solutions to them. In RET, we do not *only* or *mainly* resort to practical problem solving, but we use it *in addition to* the philosophic disputing of people's irrational beliefs.

11. *Semantic precision.* As Alfred Korzybski (1933) wisely said, people's overgeneralized and illogical thinking affects their language, and then their language encourages them to think even *more* illogically. So in RET we often question and correct the self-defeating language people use. Thus, if clients say, "I *must* perform well," we say, "No, not *must*—but *had better.*" If they say, "My mother *makes me* angry by yelling at me," we say, "No. You *anger yourself* about your mother's unfortunate yelling." If clients say, "I *can't* change my ways," we say, "*You find it difficult* to change, but there is no evidence that you *can't.*"

Transpersonal psychotherapy, then, uses insight, awareness, and other cognitive methods in limited, inefficient, and often misleading ways. Rational-emotive therapy employs a wide armamentarium of insightful and other cognitive methods while discarding the mystical, religious, and supernatural "insights" that are so dear to the hearts of transpersonalists but whose good effects are often dubious and whose potential for harm is considerable.

Almost all forms of psychotherapy attempt to eliminate people's neurotic defenses. They attempt to help clients become free of their rationalization, intellectualization, denial, hypocrisy, dishonesty, avoidance, resistance, compensation, aggression, coercion, identification, and grandiosity. Defenses may consist of unconscious defense mechanisms or may be fairly conscious. Both kinds enable people to resist acknowledging and changing self-sabotaging attitudes and actions. Rational-emotive therapists attempt to help clients surrender their defenses as well as feelings of shame, guilt, and self-deprecation that spur them to become defensive (Bernard, 1986; Ellis, 1962, 1971, 1985, 1988).

Transpersonal psychology frequently serves to bolster people's neurotic defenses by encouraging them to think nonscientifically, to set up unfalsifiable hypotheses, and to blindly endorse and profess these hypotheses as if they are unquestionably true. When shown that no evidence exists to support their theories, transpersonalists desperately resort to rationalizations, lies, hypocrisy, and hoaxes to try to substantiate them. Rather than considering alternative hypotheses to explain "supernatural" phenomena, transpersonalists tend to hold onto their theories devoutly and unyieldingly, criticize the field of science for not being "advanced" enough to understand their mystical "phenomena," and infest· their theories with a mixture of tautological reasoning and abstraction that prohibits any testing of their assumptions. For example, transpersonalists desperately try to prove the existence of magic and miracles despite a lack of substantial evidence, deny that highly dubious psychic phenomena are created by sleight of hand or optical illusion, abjure science's state-of-the-art as not capable of realistically addressing their issues, and tautologically argue that a miracle cannot be challenged. Their unwillingness to accept reality predisposes them to enlist these typical defensive postures (Kurtz, 1985a, 1986a).

Much of the core of transpersonal psychology constitutes a set of neurotic defenses against people's unwillingness to accept reality. For example, the grim reality that humans are distinctly fallible and highly limited creatures who live in a difficult and often hostile world and who are definitely, at least in this century, going to die and become nonliving and nonexistent (Ellis, 1981b, 1983b, 1986a, 1986b; Sobel, 1981) is completely dismissed by most transpersonalists. Rather, they insist that human life is eternal, thereby denying reality. They also rationalize that since this claim is not factually supportable, science has not yet advanced enough to observe immortal life. Such excuses are taught to transpersonal devotees to counter any and all arguments opposing their implausible constructs.

Besides utilizing neurotic defenses to propagate their theories, transpersonalists often soft-soap reality in a highly polyannaish manner. They assert, for example, that through prayer and spiritual enlightenment, all people can achieve "absolute peace" (Komaki, 1984, p. 3), "all wisdom and intelligence" (Dowlatashahi, 1983, p. 27), "solve the problems of any government regardless of the nature of the problem—political, economic, social, or religious" (Maharishi Mahesh Yogi, 1983a, p. A14), "bring utopia to all mankind" and perfect health and longevity to the individual and the nation (Maharishi Mahesh Yogi, 1983b, p. B20), and postpone the aging process (Silva Mind Control, 1984). They thus offer quite a kettle of grandeur! This illustrates transpersonalists' abysmally low tolerance for frustration, since it is easier for people to fabricate eternal bliss than to actually work for it!

Rational-emotive therapists directly confront people's defenses and strive to help them see the world through realistic lenses. Rather than merely distracting themselves into prayer or creating utopian pictures, RET clients learn to accept the world the way it is—and then, often, to improve it. Transpersonalists generally refuse to accept such a reality since they believe they absolutely *need* cosmic or supernatural meaning in life and *need* perfect solutions to life's problems. Such demandingness predisposes them to develop defensive views to prevent them from realizing that they will *not* likely get what they believe they need. Their defenses also help them to maintain their theories dogmatically instead of opening up and challenging them. Facts that fit their theories are accepted; those that do not are either discarded or forced to fit.

12

Aiding Short-Range Hedonism and Low Frustration Tolerance

Most responsible forms of psychotherapy help people gain greater long-range hedonistic attitudes. Rather than focusing on achievement of short-term goals or objectives, they encourage clients to gear themselves to realize long-range pleasures, even when they had better first face present hassles or discomforts to increase the probability of securing long-range rewards. As they do in most other respects, rational-emotive therapy and transpersonal psychology often differ in the importance each places on long-range hedonism.

Rational-emotive therapy firmly espouses long-range hedonism. It teaches clients to strive often for later pleasures while sacrificing some present comforts. It acknowledges that life would be easier in the here-and-now if people would live only for the moment and not be concerned with the future. However, to prioritize short-term comfort frequently maximizes long-lasting discomfort.

This is *not* to imply that RET endorses the idea of people becoming overly sacrificial so as to "ensure" later benefits. Nor is it to imply that RET holds that people *must* become long-term oriented. Rather, it asserts that a long-term orientation is *often* better, but there are no guarantees. Rational-emotive therapy duly favors here-and-now pleasures but *also* stresses long-range pursuits and teaches people how to tolerate short-term discomfort when it is likely to produce ultimate gratification.

Consider what the world would be like if all of humankind were primarily short-term focused. Few people would endure sacrifices to achieve later gains. Few people would go to college, since it is easier in the short-run to just get a job and have more money. This easy way is typical of many adolescents who do not want to tolerate frustration and delay gratification.

Again, rather than saving money or making financial investments, people would spend their money today and worry about having it tomorrow. Our divorce rate would be higher, as couples would be more oriented toward the short-term relief of their problems rather than on struggling to achieve future marital benefits. The obvious advantages of people having a more long-range attitude are many.

Although RET is frankly hedonistic in orientation, it focuses on immediate *and* long-range benefits. In fact, it holds that the central purpose in life, save survival, is enjoyment (Ellis, 1988; Ellis & Becker, 1982; Ellis & Harper, 1975). Therefore, humans had better learn to resist their innate and natural tendencies to gratify their desires immediately and to be intolerant of frustration (Ellis, 1976d, 1978, 1979a, 1980a, 1984a, 1984b, 1985, 1988; Ellis & Dryden, 1987; Ellis & Knaus, 1977). Rational-emotive therapy, therefore, endorses mottoes like, "Hard work often pays off," "Good things frequently come to those who wait," and "There's rarely any gain without pain."

While many transpersonal factions favor stoicism, "nothingness," or the "oath of poverty," some groups, such as the notable case of Bhagwan Shree Rajneesh (Lerner, 1986) and his followers, espouse the pursuit of pleasure and peace on earth. This partly agrees with the philosophy of RET, where discipline is also highly encouraged. However, transpersonal devotees often endorse unbridled pleasure (as Rajneesh often did) or else they advocate harsh discipline as an end in itself as a means by which devotees can purify their souls, rise above sensory gratification, and presumably ascend to the beatitudes of a quite nonsensual heaven.

Many transpersonalists object to the pursuit of pleasure in this lifetime. Even Rajneesh (Lerner, 1986, p. 10) renounced desire and asserted that with desirelessness "there is no need for the future." Khomeini's position regarding the pursuit of pleasure is also clear, as his devout Shiite followers uphold his prohibitions against alcohol, cosmetics, Western entertainment, and the preprogrammed Muzak (T. Smith, 1984). Similarly, the fundamentalist Christian commune Stonegate, in Jefferson County, Michigan, encourages its members to beat their children with a slim wooden rod for hours at a time for fantasizing and for minor sexual experimentation (Clendinen, 1984b). Puritanism, sexual and nonsexual, often reigns supreme in much of the transpersonal world.

In order for people to achieve long-range goals, they had better accept reasonable levels of frustration and discomfort. Rational-emotive therapy, therefore, directly promotes high frustration tolerance. Where discipline is encouraged in some transpersonal sects, it is encouraged for reasons closer to martyrdom than to long-range hedonism.

13

Aiding Authoritarianism and Blocking Human Freedom

The achievement of human freedom is another goal common to most forms of psychotherapy. A common objective is to help people become increasingly flexible and open-minded in their thinking and behaving. Although clients are encouraged to be disciplined and governed by responsible moral values, they learn that these values are often preferable guidelines for behavior, but *not* rigid and absolute dictates.

Rational-emotive therapy attempts to help people free themselves from authoritarian, fascistic, ultratraditional, ultraconforming, and ultraconservative ways of thinking and behaving. It holds that people's rigid and invariant rules for living, for themselves and others, lead not only to emotional disturbance but also to social conflict. While clients are encouraged to set long-range goals for themselves and to increase their tolerance for unavoidable frustration and discomfort, they are taught to view their goals and values as strong *preferences* and not as *absolute laws* of the universe.

Rational-emotive therapy teaches people that they can, for the most part, choose, and continue to choose, their own goals and guidelines for behavior. Although some values and mores are socially preferable and will likely help people be more happy and productive, they don't *have to* adopt such "good" values. So, too, their failure to endorse socially preferred values does not make them damnable. Rational-emotive therapy disfavors needless rules and restrictions on human thoughts and behaviors (Bernard, 1986; Ellis, 1973a, 1976d, 1979d, 1984c) while at the same time asserting a strongly prosocial attitude regarding cooperation.

Unlike rational-emotive therapy, transpersonal psychology often encourages authoritarian ideas and acts, largely due to its dogmatic allegiance to traditional mores and laws and to "sacred" scriptures. Devotees of many transpersonal sects, therefore, fail to decide their own life goals, values, and pursuits. Rather, they believe what they are instructed to believe. The transpersonal emphasis consequently reduces human freedom. It often fosters the authoritarianism of gods, high priests, and gurus (such as "leaders" like Castaneda's Don Juan [Lesser, 1984]), thereby stripping its followers of their individual freedom of choice and dictating that they blindly follow the teaching of their "superiors."

Along with transpersonal dogmatic allegiance, devout loyalty, and blind conformity, one often finds the establishment of political and religious censorship. For example, the Moslem government of Malaysia banned the New York Philharmonic from playing Ernest Bloch's *Schelomo* simply because' of its subtitle *A Hebrew Rhapsody* (Rockwell, 1984a, 1984b). Similarly, absolutistic views place and keep in power reactionary political groups such as Khomeini's Iranian regime. In their attempts to enforce rigid moral codes, transpersonalists hark back to ancient scriptures like the Bible, the Koran, the Upanishads, and the Bhagavad-Gita (Prabhupada, 1977). They deify "holy" scripture and rationalize that it is congruent with what they themselves assert. Because transpersonalists dogmatically believe that one *must* always follow such scriptures, and because their cults directly and literally spout scriptural teachings, their adherents therefore *must* obey the laws set forth by these cults.

Whereas RET favors individualistic and flexible thinking, transpersonalism maximizes devoutness, religiosity, dogmatism, and depersonalization. Rational-emotive therapy fosters both individual freedom and maximum social cooperation, whereas transpersonal thinking often fosters quite the opposite.

Some of the harm done by authoritarian religious and transpersonal cults endorsing violence, terrorism, and wars has already been described in chapter 8. Other pernicious consequences of transcendental cultism include the following:

1. Many individuals who no longer believe in cults and want to quit them or to follow less rigid pathways have been intimidated into staying and into silencing their opposition (Bishop, 1986).

2. People in nearby communities have been physically, politically, and otherwise intimidated by cult leaders and members (Gruson, 1986a, 1986b; Gordon, 1987).

3. Therapeutic cults have induced psychotherapy clients to engage in unethical and illegal acts, especially sex acts, with cult leaders (Fisher, 1985; Lewin, 1988b; Plasil, 1985).

4. Transpersonal cults have often alienated their members from their families and banned them from having any contact with other family members (Kaslow & Sussman, 1985).

5. Cults have accumulated large debts and refused to pay them off (Rajneesh Haven: A Legacy of Debts, 1988).

6. Transpersonal groups have "bullied and intimidated [people] because they weren't expressing feelings, or even because they weren't expressing the *right* feelings, such as anger" (Rowan, 1987, pp. 143–44).

7. Transpersonal sects are often patriarchal and sexist. "Most

group leaders—and a bigger majority of the best paid and most prestigious leaders—are men. And most group leaders (in all the cases I have seen where any statistics have been kept) are men" (Rowan, 1987, p. 151; L. Harris, 1985).

8. Many of the transpersonal leaders who preach love and peace are hostile, vindictive individuals (Gordon, 1987; Yeats, 1986).

9. Religious and transpersonal cults powerfully indoctrinate group members with anti-individualistic, guilt-inducing attitudes that lead to depression and self-denigration (Luce, 1986).

10. Some transcendental and fundamentalist cult members are being bilked of their savings and intimidated into making contributions to these cults (Brooks, 1986).

11. Censorship and book burning is rife among fundamentalist cults (Luce, 1986). In the United States, Christian fundamentalists have tried for many years to ban scientific texts that conflict with biblical teachings and to force science teachers to promulgate Judeo-Christian views as well. Although the courts have struck down several statutes that would have mandated fundamentalist teachings about creationism in our school curricula, fundamentalist efforts to censor scientific texts still have a powerful influence on textbook publishers (Gould, 1987; Seckel, 1986–87). John Baker (1986), whom we quoted at the end of chapter 8, notes in this respect, that the chaos resulting from this kind of simplistic thinking and intolerance could easily lead to a new dark age.

Again, we do not want to neglect the fact that many transpersonal leaders and groups sometimes abet freedom and individualism. We still hold that any group whose members believe in an intuitively derived Absolute Truth is more likely than not to favor and foster authoritarian attitudes and practices. This authoritarianism will frequently lead to the kind of coercive, censorious, and antihumane practices that have been inflicted on members (and outsiders) of a large number of "spiritual" groups.

Increased social interest is sought by most forms of psychotherapy. Whereas the psychotherapeutic emphasis is typically placed on helping people increase their self-interest, it is concomitantly placed on minimizing their antisocialness. Clients are generally encouraged to become interested in cooperating with their fellow inhabitants and in preserving planetary resources.

Rational-emotive therapy tries to help people strike a balance between self-interest and social interest (Bernard, 1986; Ellis, 1973a, 1984a, 1985, 1988; Ellis & Becker, 1982; Ellis & Harper, 1975). In this respect, it largely endorses the views of Alfred Adler (1964) and helps people become interested in others while simultaneously remaining sufficiently interested in themselves so as not to be overly sacrificial or martyrlike.

Transpersonal psychology often helps people to be so autistic and so self-centered that they are not really interested in the well-being of their fellow humans. Instead, they frequently are driven into devotion to God, to worship of the Absolute, to fanatical homage to the rituals of their transpersonal sect, to prayer, and to delusionary unity with the inanimate world. While RET helps people to be interested in the welfare of society at large, transpersonalists attempt to bias their followers toward nonhumanistic and superhuman interests (Bhatty, 1984a, 1984b; Breutsch, 1984; E. Brown, 1984; Cohn, 1983; Franklyn, 1973; Kurtz, 1985a, 1986a; G. H. Smith, 1979; Tart, 1975; Yale, 1984).

Transpersonal psychology's beliefs in karma and fatalism also seriously interfere with social action for betterment. Atheists like Jean-Paul Sartre (1968) and Bertrand Russell (1965), once they see that life has no intrinsic meaning and that the universe appears to have no interest whatsoever in helping or hindering humans, frequently decide to *give* their lives meaning by engaging in social activism and fighting against political oppression and warfare (Griffin, 1984). However, the transpersonalist and neo-Hegelian notion that "there is a higher level of reality and a Divine Purpose to all that happens" (Breutsch, 1984, p. 24) maintains an attitude of social complacency. This attitude may also lead to a condemnation of those who espouse differing views and a force feeding of these "godly" values to others through violence and oppression (see chapter 8).

Abetting self-interest is a common goal in psychotherapy. This is not to say that therapists strive to help their clients to become overly self-indulgent, smug, self-righteous, or uninterested in the welfare of others. On the contrary, self-interest does not mean self*ish*. Rather, it implies helping oneself to happiness but *also* being interested in others' welfare. Social interest does not imply becoming the sacrificial lamb for others or finding the Gates of Heaven through the path of martyrdom. To be self-interested is to be geared toward benefitting one's self while maintaining a strong interest in the social group in which this self *chooses* to live.

Rational-emotive therapy hypothesizes that mentally adjusted or "healthy" individuals have considerable social concern and are considerate and fair to others. So, too, they neither sacrifice themselves unduly for other people nor immolate themselves completely for various causes (Ellis, 1962, 1965; Ellis & Becker, 1982; Ellis & Harper, 1975). Although RET considers helping others to be adaptive behavior, to do so at the expense of satisfying one's own strong desires is often harmful. "Healthy" people, therefore, are considered to be those who are neither autistically self*ish* nor overly self-sacrificing.

Transpersonal psychology abets errant self-sacrifice by encouraging its devotees to give their all for God, for natural law, for their cult, and for their supposedly godlike leader (Bhatty, 1984a; McAleavy, 1983; Maharishi Mahesh Yogi, 1982; Read, 1983). As Sri Swami Rama (1982, p. 3) states, "the moment one becomes selfish, the mind changes its course and starts flowing downward to the lower grooves." Statements like these confuse "selfishness" (doing others in) with self-interest (helping oneself).

When people think and behave self-interestedly, they experience greater pleasures and rewards in life. They commonly develop increased personal mastery and self-efficacy, leading to improved mood productivity. Rational-emotive therapy encourages clients to be self-interested *and* to benefit their fellow humans. The transpersonal belief that one must not take an interest in one's self unless one "deservingly" merits mystical grace leads to subservience, emotional disturbance, and lack of fulfillment.

14

Refusing to Accept the Inevitable

Helping people to accept (not necessarily *like*) the inevitable is another common goal of psychotherapy. Achieving such acceptance helps them reduce their misery about poor but unchangeable life circumstances. Rather than making themselves depressed over their mortality, for example, clients are encouraged to accept this fact of life and still make the best out of their existence. Whereas transpersonal psychologists sometimes do emphasize acceptance of the inevitable, they differ from other forms of psychotherapy in two distinct ways.

First, transpersonal psychology often biases clients to believe in an "inevitability" that is anti-empirical and highly unlikely. It claims, with absolute conviction and assuredness, that an inevitable peace or unity is destined for all who obey the commandments of the cult. But, rather than formulating or articulating its theories of salvation as hypotheses or beliefs, TP dogmatically and unscrutinizingly maintains that if the client chooses the right path, he will realize eternal bliss. This seems highly dubious!

The second point where TP differs from RET and most other therapies with respect to inevitability is its endorsement of fatalistic views. Whereas most schools of thought help people change unpleasant life circumstances, transpersonalists promulgate a strong belief in karma and often lead their followers to self-defeating passivity and lack of social and individual action (Rama, 1982). Transpersonalists assert that humans are unquestionably ruled by forces outside or beyond them, and that divergence from the prescriptions of these forces is impossible, thus exacerbating people's *passive* tolerance of unfortunate life events.

Rational-emotive therapy holds to the views of Saint Francis, Reinhold Niebuhr, and Alcoholics Anonymous—all of whom help people toward realistic *acceptance* of life situations that are unchangeable. Contrary to transpersonalist contentions, however, RET maintains that it is often possible to change unpleasant circumstances rather than passively succumbing to them. How? By reducing disturbance and resorting to hard work (Ellis, 1962, 1973a, 1979a, 1980a, 1984a, 1987a, 1988; Ellis & Dryden, 1987; Ellis & Grieger, 1986; Ellis & Harper, 1975).

Acceptance of unchangeable, unpleasant activating events after trying hard to alter them is a major goal of RET. Transpersonal psychology, on the other hand, fosters the nonacceptance of reality in several more ways:

1. It encourages the creation and endorsement of ancient and modern myths, fairy tales, and magical solutions to serious problems. As A. Agena (1983, p. 180) observes: "The emergence of archaic, mystical motifs in the culture today represents a groping effort to find a replacement for the world view we have lost. But it does not work."

2. Transpersonal psychology, by escaping into Abraham Maslow's "fourth force," tends to build "a psychology without people in it" (Gregory Bateson, quoted in May, 1986).

3. Transpersonalists like Marilyn Ferguson (1980) invent an "Aquarian Conspiracy" that is unrealistic and utopian and that lacks the ability to *change* grim reality (Michael, 1985).

4. Transpersonalists are often pollyannas who will not face, accept, or work to change such negative aspects of human nature as cruelty, anxiety, and evil (May, 1986).

5. Transpersonal psychology assumes that we cannot use our humanity to help ourselves improve our social interest but instead need transcendental or suprahuman powers to do this (Valle, 1986). Quite a defeatist position!

6. Transpersonalists simply will not accept the obvious reality that, so far, all living things, including humans, die and stay dead. They invent reincarnation, and are absolutely sure that an afterlife exists and that their immortal souls will go marching on forever (Cardinal, 1986a, 1988a; Katz, 1982; McDermott, 1986; White, 1987; Woolger, 1986). Although there is no evidence whatever of reincarnation and considerable data showing the spurious nature of self-reported reincarnation experiences (Conn, 1988; Edwards, 1987; Wilson, 1982), devout belief in its "proof" is held by innumerable transpersonalists.

7. In advocating selflessness or self-negation (Fontana, 1987), transpersonal psychology amazingly refuses to acknowledge that this can only be achieved, if at all, by personal choice and hard work. It takes a "self" to deny a "self" or to *choose* "oneness with the universe." Once again, TP stubbornly refuses to accept reality!

8. In spite of an incredible amount of evidence against unidentified flying objects and people from outer space, transpersonalists devoutly believe in, and actually "observe," such extraterrestrials—and then, in a paranoid fashion, invent the aliens' pernicious influence on earthly affairs (Montgomery, 1985).

15

Favoring Ineffective
Psychotherapy Techniques

The specific therapeutic strategies endorsed by various schools of psychology are derived from the theory and goals of the particular school being discussed. As rational-emotive therapy and transpersonal psychotherapy differ drastically in both their philosophic underpinnings and treatment goals, so, too, do their therapeutic strategies and methods. Let us now consider some of their main differences in regard to techniques of psychotherapy.

LACK OF BEHAVIORAL EMPHASIS

Rational-emotive therapy and transpersonal psychotherapy differ in their respective endorsements of the importance of behavioral methods of change. Although RET is one of the most cognitive and philosophic of all of the current psychotherapies, it holds that deep and lasting emotional changes rarely take place unless clients not only think scientifically but also *act* forcefully and repetitively against their disturbed thoughts and feelings. Consequently, RET has always favored activity homework assignments and desensitization by facing live dangers as two of its main techniques (Bernard, 1986; Ellis, 1956, 1962, 1969a, 1969b, 1973a, 1988; Ellis & Abrahams, 1978; Ellis & Becker, 1982; Ellis & Bernard, 1983, 1985; Ellis & Dryden, 1987; Ellis & Grieger, 1986; Ellis & Whiteley, 1979).

Some of the main behavioral methods steadily used in RET include:

1. *Cognitive homework assignments.* Clients are asked to make lists of current problems, look for their irrational beliefs that largely create these problems, dispute these beliefs, and fill out RET self-help reports (Sichel & Ellis, 1983) that help them structure their irrational beliefs and their disputations of these dysfunctional ideas.

2. *Activity homework assignments.* Clients devise with their therapists desensitizing assignments pertinent to their life situations, wherein they risk doing things they are irrationally afraid to do, they stay in uncomfortable and "awful" situations until they become comfortable (or even happy) with them, and they overcome their compulsions and addictions by different kinds of response prevention.

3. *Gradual and implosive desensitizing activities.* Rational-emotive therapy clients are not only encouraged to desensitize themselves gradually to their irrational fears and phobias but also, at times, implosively, in rapid succession to perform tasks that they dread doing, so that they quickly and strongly overcome their needless anxieties. Rational-emotive therapy does not require, but often recommends, rapid desensitizing behaviors.

4. *Skill training.* Partly because it stemmed from my pioneering use of active-directive sex therapy (Ellis, 1954) and of assertion training (Ellis, 1963), RET has always included skill training. While helping clients change their irrational Beliefs (at point

B) and modify their emotional and behavioral Consequences (at point C), RET practitioners also bring clients back to the Activating Events (at point A) in their lives and show them how to acquire practical skills that they may lack—skills at communication, at relating intimately, at having satisfying sex, at job seeking and business relations, and at time management.

5. *Reinforcement and penalizing.* To help them do their cognitive, emotive, and behavioral homework assignments, RET clients are shown how to reinforce themselves when they carry out their self-changes and how to penalize themselves when they fail to do so (Ellis & Knaus, 1977; Ellis & Whiteley, 1979).

6. *Physical methods of therapy.* Although RET does not glorify body work and takes a skeptical view of creating emotional miracles by body massage and manipulation, it frequently encourages its clients to use health-abetting exercise, proper nutrition, relaxation, biofeedback, and other physical techniques when these seem beneficial. It hardly endorses the view that all physical ills are psychologically caused, or that all mental and emotional aberrations have a clear-cut biochemical basis. But it frequently recommends a combination of cognitive-behavioral methods accompanied by suitable psychotropic medication for individuals with severe neurotic, borderline, and psychotic problems.

Unlike RET, transpersonal psychology ignores the most effective behavioral methods of therapy and instead often prescribes ritualistic activities (such as frenzied chanting, dancing, praying, and incantations) that at times may offer temporary distraction from anxiety and depression but are not scientifically designed to change dysfunctional behaviors permanently. Moreover, these behavioral aspects of transpersonal psychology frequently *add* needless burdens and compulsions to disturbed people's lives.

Especially in its transcendental form, transpersonal psychology largely sticks to cognitive, meditative, suggestive, and other thinking and experiential methods of change. It often fails to employ planned and structured behavioral programs designed to alleviate specific phobias, obsessions, compulsions, and other symptoms of disturbance. When behavioral methods such as yoga exercises are employed, they are often converted into compulsive rituals.

The psychotherapeutic literature is replete with studies showing the efficacy of behavioral strategies with people displaying a wide range of personal and interpersonal difficulties. In fact, several behavioral strategies may be employed when specific disorders are present (Bellack & Hersen, 1985).

The harmful effects of many of transpersonal psychology's prescribed behavioral methods are often overlooked. For example, transpersonalists typically fail to address the back and neck injuries that yoga headstands often cause, and the serious health problems associated with extreme dieting and fasting that are commonly encouraged.

Where RET favors behavioral methods to aid and reinforce profound philosophic change, transpersonal psychotherapy often prescribes behavioral methods such as compulsive rituals as ends in themselves. Where modern cognitive behavioral therapy tests its methods vigorously and discards those that do not work (Bandura, 1977; Beck, 1976; Bellack & Hersen, 1985; Bernard & DiGiuseppe, 1988; Kazdin, 1978; Kazdin & Wilson, 1978; Mahoney, 1974; Meichenbaum, 1977), transpersonal psychotherapy adopts behavioral methods on magical or mystical grounds.

LACK OF EFFECTIVE EMOTIVE TECHNIQUES

Rational-emotive therapy and transpersonal psychotherapy also differ in the importance placed on the emotive aspects of therapy. As the name rational-*emotive* therapy implies, RET has always focused on human emotions and emotional disturbance. In addition to cognitive and behavioral intervention strategies, it includes a number of highly evocative, dramatic, and forceful techniques (Bernard, 1986; Dryden, 1984; Ellis, 1971, 1972a, 1973a, 1976b, 1977a, 1977b, 1977c, 1979a, 1979b, 1987a, 1987e, 1988, 1989; Ellis & Abrahms, 1978; Ellis & Becker, 1982; Ellis & Bernard, 1983, 1985; Ellis & Dryden, 1987; Ellis & Grieger, 1986; Maultsby & Ellis, 1974).

Although RET is unusually cognitive and philosophic, it theorizes that when people have what we call "emotional" disturbances, and especially when they have trouble surrendering their severe feelings of anxiety, depression, rage, and worthlessness, they create and bolster these feelings with irrational beliefs that they hold very *strongly* or *forcefully*. Consequently, to change or eliminate these beliefs, they often had better dispute them *powerfully* and *vigorously* and replace them with *firmly held* rational ideas.

Therefore, RET uses with most clients a number of highly emotive, evocative, and dramatic methods such as:

1. *Forceful coping statements.* Therapists help clients to formulate rational self-statements or coping statements and to say these to themselves many times in a powerful, forceful manner. For example: "I do NOT need people's approval, but *only* desire it! I CAN stand it when significant others disapprove of me! It's NOT awful and terrible but MERELY an inconvenience. And I can definitely accept and enjoy myself *even* when someone I care for *doesn't* like me!"

2. *Rational emotive imagery.* Rational-emotive therapy uses a modified, more emotive form of Maultsby's (Maultsby & Ellis, 1974) rational-emotive imagery. Clients are shown how they can vividly imagine one of the worst things that may happen to them (such as being constantly criticized by a boss or a mate), how they can let themselves feel inappropriately upset (such as feeling very depressed or angry) about this, how to

implode this feeling and really experience it, and then how to change it to an appropriate feeling (such as feeling sorry, disappointed, or frustrated). When they do so, they are shown a way to discover *how* they changed their feeling (that is, by giving up their *musts* and *demands* and instead holding on to only their *wishes* and *preferences*). They then keep practicing this procedure for thirty to sixty days, until they start automatically to feel sorry and disappointed rather than depressed and angry when they imagine this bad thing happening, or when it actually occurs.

3. *Unconditional acceptance.* Rational-emotive therapists do their best to *un*conditionally accept their clients, even when these clients exhibit stupid or reprehensible behavior; and the therapists model this kind of acceptance in their tone and behavior. But, unlike the followers of Carl Rogers (1961), they also actively *teach* their clients how to accept themselves and others without damnation.

4. *Role-playing.* Therapists often role-play difficult situations (such as being interviewed for a job) with their clients, and thereby not only provide clients with behavioral rehearsal, but also evoke these disturbed feelings. Rational-emotive therapy uses role-playing in this manner but additionally interrupts the role-play to show clients what they are telling themselves to create in their disturbances, and what they can do to change their inappropriate feelings to appropriate ones.

5. *Forceful dialogues.* Clients are shown how to conduct dialogues with themselves in which they express their irrational beliefs and then powerfully dispute them. These self-dialogues are recorded and then replayed so that the therapist can discover exactly how convincingly—and how *strongly*—the clients argued against their irrational philosophies. At times, reverse role-playing is done, with the RET practitioner vigorously

upholding the client's self-defeating ideas and the client being required to vigorously talk the therapist out of these dysfunctional notions.

6. *Shame-attacking exercises.* When, as is often true, clients have a dire need for the approval of others and feel ashamed of doing what they really want to do out of fear of disapproval, they are given RET's famous shame-attacking exercises. Thus, they accept the assignment of going out in public, doing something foolish or ridiculous (like singing at the top of their lungs or asking a silly question at a lecture), and working on themselves so that they do *not* feel ashamed, embarrassed, or humiliated (Ellis, 1969b, 1972a, 1988). They keep doing these exercises until they see that their feelings of shame are self-created and do not really stem from the "embarrassing" situation, and until they become considerably less inhibited and ashamed.

7. *Humor.* While RET helps people take seriously the unfortunate or undesirable events of their lives, and make concerted efforts to change what they can change, it holds that neurotic disturbances often arise from taking things *too* seriously and losing one's sense of humor about them. Consequently, RET uses humor and laughter to counterattack people's overseriousness and to help them dispute their dogmatic *musts* and their disturbance-creating absolutistic thinking (Ellis, 1977b). It frequently employs rational, humorous songs (Ellis, 1977c), which it encourages people to sing to themselves (or in groups) when they feel anxious, depressed, enraged, or self-denigrating. Here, for example are some typical RET songs:

WHINE, WHINE, WHINE! (Tune: Yale's "Whiffenpoof Song" by Guy Scull—a Harvard man!)

> I cannot have all of my wishes filled—
> Whine, whine, whine!
> I cannot have every frustration stilled—
> Whine, whine, whine!
> Life really owes me the things that I miss,
> Fate has to grant me eternal bliss!
> Since I must settle for less than this—
> Whine, whine, whine!

PERFECT RATIONALITY (Tune: "Funiculi, Funicula" by Luigi Denza)

> Some think the world must have a right direction,
> And so do I! And so do I!
> Some think that, with the slightest imperfection,
> They can't get by—and so do I!
> For I, I have to prove I'm superhuman,
> And better far than people are!
> To show I have miraculous acumen—
> And always rate among the Great!
>
> Perfect, perfect rationality
> Is, of course, the only thing for me!
> How can I ever think of being
> If I must live fallibly?
> Rationality must be a perfect thing for me!

LOVE ME, LOVE ME, ONLY ME! (Tune: "Yankee Doodle")

> Love me, love me, only me
> Or I'll die without you!
> Make your love a guarantee,
> So I can never doubt you!
> Love me, love me totally—really, really try, dear.
> But if you demand love, too,
> I'll hate you till I die, dear!

Love me, love me all the time,
Thoroughly and wholly!
Life turns into slushy slime
'Less you love me solely!
Love me with great tenderness,
With no ifs or buts, dear.
If you love me somewhat less,
I'll hate your goddamned guts, dear!

(Lyrics by Albert Ellis, copyright © 1977 by
Institute for Rational-Emotive Therapy)

Although RET commonly employs many emotive, forceful therapeutic strategies such as those just described, it is highly selective
and discriminating in its employment of these techniques. It is also
skeptical of the effectiveness and potential iatrogenic effects of many
commonly employed emotive methods. For example, RET questions
the utility of encouraging the deliberate escalation and expression of
anger and the overt expression of love by therapists for their clients.
These and other questionable techniques are often enthusiastically
endorsed by transpersonal and other therapies (Ellis, 1985, 1986a).

In employing emotive methods, transpersonalists have no one
viewpoint but rather include both extremes of the evocative conti-
nuum. Some transpersonal sects abjure many of the important emotive
aspects of psychotherapy and, instead, concentrate almost exclusively
on pure contemplation, meditation, and prayer. They tend to favor
extreme Stoicism rather than helping humans maximize their emotional happiness. They do not stress feeling better, but feeling nothing.

On the opposite extreme, transpersonalists such as devotees of
Sufism, Hare Krishna, and the Rajneesh sponsor emotive outbursts
that border on the psychotic and that often drive some of them tem-
porarily over the edge. Rather than endorsing the purging of emotions,
RET tries to help people to experience their emotions better and to
learn how to manage these emotions. While RET includes strategies

aimed at giving clients better emotional education so that they can identify their emotions and know and sometimes change what they feel, transpersonalists often view "getting in touch with one's feelings" or "experiencing feelings" as ends in and of themselves. This means, RET hypothesizes, that clients will likely learn how to experience and live with their more disturbed feelings when they had better not only "know" these feelings but also know how to change them. Contrarily, transpersonalists often encourage emotional instability by their fanatical devotion to religious causes such as those of the Moonies, the Jim Jones cult, the Maharishi, and *est* (Ellis, 1986b).

Rational-emotive therapy clearly differentiates between inappropriate and self-defeating feelings (such as rage, anxiety, depression, shame, and extreme guilt) and appropriate and self-helping feelings (such as annoyance, concern, sadness, and disappointment). Transpersonal psychology, however, does not. Peculiarly and contradictorily enough, while transpersonal psychology ostensibly advocates the most contemplative and often schizoid kind of "higher" existence, it at times deifies emotional and experiential processes and makes them the very core of "higher" mystical knowledge (E. Brown, 1984; Ferguson, 1980; Houston, 1982; Mann, 1984; Moss & Hosford, 1983; Lerner, 1986; Shah, 1982; Tulku, 1977, 1978). Rational-emotive therapy, on the other hand, strives to maximize the clients' happiness while minimizing the extent to which they experience inappropriate and self-defeating emotions.

Rational-emotive therapy employs emotive and evocative techniques within therapy sessions and as real life homework assignments. However, it does not prescribe such strategies solely because of their intrinsic appeal or to help clients get their feelings "out," but to help them *change* some of their thoughts, emotions, and actions. It also holds that the mere purging of emotions is likely to be more iatrogenic than productive.

Clients will often utilize their therapy sessions as models to help themselves behave differently when their therapists are not available.

If they learn in transpersonal therapy that they "feel better" through cathartically purging their feelings, they are likely to employ that strategy by themselves. Because, however, their friends, relatives, and associates will probably be unreceptive to this kind of socially unappealing catharsis, they can easily alienate their peers and exacerbate their interpersonal problems. Rational-emotive therapy, therefore, tries to employ emotive procedures that can also be useful in the outside life of clients.

Rational-emotive therapy's evocative procedures can also be helpful with clients who are loath to divulge personal information or share their feelings or beliefs. Thus, if an emotional response is evoked in a therapy session, clients will be more likely to indicate what bothers them. Once their irrational beliefs are activated with an emotive strategy, these are "ripe for the pickings" and available for disputation.

Employment of evocative procedures is also quite useful with clients who are hyperfearful of their own feelings. This is very common when working with alcohol- or substance abusing-individuals (Ellis, 1978; Ellis, McInerney, DiGiuseppe & Yeager, 1988) and children of alcoholics. By evoking an emotional reaction from these clients, RET therapists can help them reconstruct their belief that their experiences are *too* uncomfortable or painful to face. Similarly, as the client fears of emotion are extinguished by concluding that their feelings *are,* in fact, tolerable, the therapist can prescribe exercises to aid acceptance of emotion outside of the therapy session.

The utility of emotive therapeutic strategies is potentially great. Transpersonal therapies that dismiss these techniques or take them to extremes ignore the scientific therapy literature and sabotage their own effectiveness.

LACK OF RELATIONSHIP ENHANCEMENT

Helping people to enhance their interpersonal relationships is another means through which clients are helped to achieve their long-term personal goals. This is not to say that people "need" others, but to contend that it is "preferable" that they relate better. Humans are gregarious animals (Aronson, 1976), and it is best to help them realize their social potential.

Rational-emotive therapy strives to enhance human relationships in many ways. To do this, it teaches people that they are always unconditionally acceptable and are never to be denigrated or damned, by either themselves or others, for anything that they do or fail to do (Ellis, 1962, 1972a, 1972b, 1973a, 1976c, 1976d, 1979d, 1984c, 1987a, 1987b, 1987e, 1988). They thereby tend to become increasingly tolerant and understanding of the ways of others and to bring about increased social cooperation.

RET directly shows people how to better relate with others and to do so with minimal anger and conflict (Ellis, 1957, 1975b, 1977a, 1979d; Ellis & Becker, 1982; Ellis & Harper, 1961, 1975). It also teaches clients such relating skills as how to be more assertive, how to better communicate with others, how to maximize one's sexual pleasures, and how to be patient and cooperative in working with others (Crawford, 1982; Ellis, 1956, 1975b, 1976c, 1977f, 1979d, 1981a, 1986c; Lacey, 1982; Lange & Jakubowski, 1976). In essence, RET helps people learn how to work better and play well with others.

Unlike rational-emotive therapy, transpersonal psychotherapy fosters more of an autistic rather than a social orientation. Rather than focusing on helping their clients relate with each other better, transpersonalists help these people relate more intimately with their inner souls, with the inanimate universe, with the Absolute, and with God (Deikman, 1972, 1982; Stace, 1960). As a result, transpersonal psychology frequently augments people's schizoid detachment from others (Bhatty, 1983, 1984a; Ellis, 1983b, 1983c, 1984d, 1985, 1986b; Parsons & Wicks, 1986; Zindler, 1988) and suppresses their biological and sociological predisposition for gregariousness.

Whereas it can be rationally argued that people can benefit from becoming increasingly aware of their thoughts, feelings, and inner values, and whereas they may productively acquire insight into their motivations, it is likely that total introspection and the exclusion of developing good working relations with others is more harmful than helpful. As a result, through transpersonal inner-absorption, people come to deny the importance of others and often become narcissistically asocial, and even antisocially oriented.

LACK OF SELF-HELP EMPHASIS

Therapies that foster self-direction and independence are considered to be most responsible from a humanistic perspective (Ellis, 1973a, 1983a). Consequently, RET endorses a self-help model and teaches people to achieve maximum self-direction and independent thinking. Rather than encouraging people to be overly beholden to others and to be dependent on external conditions, RET directly helps them to determine and follow their own responses and directions. Clients are, therefore, shown how to reconstruct their ideas, emotions, and behaviors so as to avoid *too much* social conformity, to rely only moderately on a therapist, to keep striving to *be* themselves rather than to *prove* themselves, and to avoid undue habituation, automaticity, and conditioning (Bernard, 1986; Ellis, 1962, 1971, 1973a, 1987a, 1987b, 1988; Ellis & Becker, 1982; Ellis & Bernard, 1983, 1985). Even when it uses reinforcement and behavioral conditioning procedures, RET avoids leading clients into unthinking robotism (Ellis, 1983d).

Rather than espousing a self-help perspective, transpersonal psychotherapy fosters dependence on a "leader," whether it be an idol, a king, an ideology, or a psychotherapist. Independence is stifled. Transpersonal psychology often urges clients to become dependent on dogmas, gods, and gurus (Breutsch, 1984; Harman, 1981). Rather than helping clients to function with increased independence, it tells them that they must tap into Universal Energy and Light. Senseless rituals and rigamaroles are prescribed and transpersonal devotees become convinced that these rites must be rigidly followed. Similarly, a devout reliance on prayer (Ellis, 1983c; Harper, 1983) and on fanatical support groups (such as the Moonies) is encouraged.

Transpersonal devotees are also convinced that they must swear undying devotion (or dying devotion, as was the case with the suicidal followers of Jim Jones) to a supposedly divine and faultless leader (McAleavy, 1983; Wykert, 1975). As McCorkle (1969, p. 146) has stated in his endorsement of transpersonal psychology: "The true letting go, the one that is surrender, is the abandonment of self-control to the divine source of our being, in faith that it will lead us to our own supreme good."

Rational-emotive therapy differs from transpersonal psychology and from many other forms of psychotherapy by discouraging dependence in several ways:

1. It directly engages clients in self-help procedures, such as generating their own homework assignments.

2. It engages clients in self-monitoring strategies.

3. It teaches clients that they are controlled not by outside activating events, but rather by the views that they take of them.

4. It teaches clients that they can change their emotional and behavioral responses to the world by restructuring the ways in which they perceive, interpret, and evaluate this world.

5. It directly contradicts clients' beliefs that they *need* their therapist and will likely always need him or her.

Whereas transpersonal psychotherapy produces high levels of dependence, rational-emotive therapy abets personal independence.

LACK OF SELF-CONTROL EMPHASIS

Self-control strategies are becoming increasingly more popular across schools of psychotherapy. Despite skepticism of some therapists, self-control procedures have "become a respectable enterprise" (Rimm & Masters, 1979, p. 422).

Like behavior therapy, RET stresses the virtue of self-control and teaches clients methods of choosing their own thoughts, feelings, and actions (Ellis, 1979a, 1980a, 1983a, 1983b, 1985, 1988). Clients learn how to engage in self-monitoring and self-reinforcement, rather than relying on others or outside events to determine their "destinies." For example, RET helps clients outline contingency contracts for themselves, engage in self-directed relaxation or biofeedback therapy, and direct their own life experiments. The RET model, therefore, is clearly one that is geared toward increasing self-help.

Not unlike RET, transpersonal psychotherapists do teach some forms of self-control, such as meditation, yoga, and breathing exercises. However, the abandonment of self-control is also often encouraged. As McCorkle (1969, p. 146) again states, transpersonalists advocate "the abandonment of self-control to the divine source of our being, in faith that it will lead us to our own supreme good." Moreover, they strongly imply that rather than persistently engaging in self-training, merely getting in touch with the supreme Unity of things will itself automatically lead to being in full command of oneself (Brown, 1984; Deikman, 1982; Osborne & Baldwin, 1982; Tannous, 1983; Wilber, 1982a, 1982c).

Whereas RET teaches clients not only self-direction but also self-control, transpersonal psychology favors giving up one's freedom and independence in favor of becoming passive and dependent on gods, rules, or leaders for ultimate betterment. Rational-emotive therapy invites action and teaches people that they are not the passive victims of life's activating events. In RET therapy, clients develop an armamentarium of skills, which they are continually encouraged to practice, to increase their abilities to respond to the world. They therefore feel less out of control and are less likely to respond reflexively to outside stimuli. This typically results in increased confidence and decreased fear. But as a result of the transpersonal inclination to give up control to a Higher Power, people often feel out of control, fail to take responsibility for their actions, and claim that disturbances are the result of fate, karma, or God's will.

LACK OF EMPHASIS ON CLIENT COMMITMENT

Helping people to become committed to certain vital, absorbing life interests is another means through which therapists can help them overcome much of their emotional distress (Ellis & Harper, 1975). This is congruent with the theory that asserts that depression largely stems from people having insufficient reinforcement in their lives (Lewinsohn, 1974). Similarly, some interpersonal psychotherapists (e.g., Klerman et al., 1979) attempt to help clients achieve greater social reinforcement. Cognitive therapists also encourage their clients to become increasingly active so as to maximize their experiences and pleasures (Beck, 1976; Beck, Rush, Shaw & Emery, 1979; Ellis, 1979d, 1985, 1987a, 1988).

A person's active and persistent engagement in vital, absorbing interests can include having a long-term career, raising a family, devotion to a cause, or involvement in some intense hobby. Rational-emotive therapy shows clients how to select their own interests or causes while *not* developing obsessive-compulsive addictions (Ellis & Becker, 1982; Ellis & Harper, 1975; Ellis, McInerney, DiGiuseppe & Yeager, 1988). A clear distinction is made between appreciating such "passions" and irrationally believing that one *must* be totally impassioned.

Transpersonal psychology also favors the passionate pursuit of a cause. However, it endeavors to induce its adherents to become thoroughly obsessed and compulsively involved in a single supreme cause, such as becoming fanatical subscribers to Unity, to the Absolute, and to Higher Consciousness (Bugental, 1971; Deikman, 1982; Ferguson, 1980; Hammer, 1971; Mann, 1984; Stace, 1960). Devotees of transpersonal sects, therefore, often become anonymous, mindless followers who are oneness-directed or spirit-directed. Their fanaticism monolithically rules their lives, shuts out many other enjoyable possibilities, and blocks their commitment to other meaningful, and less frantic, pursuits.

USE OF FANATICAL HEALTH AND HEALING METHODS

Health-improvement strategies are recommended by most schools of psychotherapy. Rational-emotive therapy holds that emotional upsets often tend to cause or even exacerbate physical ailments. Similarly, somatic problems often lead to or aggravate one's emotional difficulties (Ellis, 1988; Ellis & Dryden, 1987).

In an effort to maximize personal happiness and increase long-term goal production, RET encourages people to manage their physical health better and to get into good condition (Ellis, 1983a; Witkin, 1985). It, therefore, aids them in giving up smoking, drugs, alcohol (Ellis, 1976d, 1978; Ellis, McInerney, DiGiuseppe, & Yeager, 1988), overeating, and avoidance of exercise. It also encourages people to relieve their emotional distresses to minimize the somatic disabilities often associated with stress.

Whereas RET helps people achieve good physical health, it does not deify the importance of body work, holistic health maintenance, or other health-abetting activities. As it combats fanaticism of all kinds, so, too, it discourages health fanaticism (Witkin, 1985) as this is also likely lead to further health risks.

The transpersonal perspective on health is often quite frenetic, rigid, and compulsive. Probably because of its sanctification of direct experience, its extremist tendencies, and its enormous reluctance to check any theory with scientific investigations, transpersonal psychology subscribes to health views and practices that are often fanatical, particularly some aspects of "holistic medicine."

Transpersonalists frequently sanctify body work, asserting that it, by itself, will change an individual's disturbances. Transpersonalists often ignore the biochemical changes that occur as a result of improved fitness, and the restructured *beliefs* people tend to develop about themselves and their worlds as a result of being more fit. Instead, transpersonalists tend to deify fitness and dismiss psychological variables that may contribute to personality changes.

Transpersonalists employ various "medical" practices that often border on the bizarre. A prime example is their endorsement of shamanism and faith-healing. In attempting to explain the mechanisms through which faith-healing works, they ignore that what passes for occasional effectiveness stems from people's *belief* in it, and not from the shamans and faith-healer's possession of real magical powers. On the contrary, transpersonalists claim that shamans do have such miraculous abilities (Calderon, Cowan, Sharon & Sharon, 1982; Enelow, cited in Colodzin, 1983; Fairfield, 1984; R. Katz, 1982; MacDougall, 1983; Raphael, 1982). They ignore the investigations of Levinthal (1983) and others that provide evidence for a natural explanation of shamanism and faith-healing.

Some of the claims of the faith-healers are, to say the least, extravagant; so far not one of them has been backed by valid scientific investigations (Kurtz, 1986b). On the other hand, many of their claims have been shown to be invalid or fraudulent (Barnhardt, 1986; Fowler & Crawford, 1988; Kurtz, 1986b, 1986c; Randi, 1986a, 1986b, 1987; Singer, 1986; Stalker & Glymour, 1985). Some of the best known "God-inspired" healers—such as Billy Hargis, Jimmy Swaggart, and Tammy and Jim Bakker—have been caught in sexual and other offenses that were clearly forbidden to their followers. Many of them have amassed huge fortunes from their radio and television evangelistic appeals, and several have lived in obvious luxury as a result of their successful "godly" pursuits. Pat Robertson, for example, is said to have collected 250 million dollars in 1985 for his fundamentalist Christian Broadcasting 700 Club.

Some of the fairly common claims of various faith-healers—most of which differ fascinatingly from each other!—include the following:

You can use "channeling" by employing your body as a conduit to get in touch with and tap the healing wisdom of spiritual beings, most of whom have been dead for centuries (Golin, 1988).

Through Katsugen (also known as Rei-do), or moving Zen, and by yawning, stretching, and massaging your eyes, you can "improve your balance and healing ability and enhance the quality of your *ki* (life force)" (Yamamoto, 1988, p. 14).

You can use Ayurvedic medicine, "with special emphasis on herbs and spices easily available in the kitchen. The Ayurvedic approach to specific diseases such as rheumatism will be presented, followed by the concept of rejuvenation" (Svoboda, 1988, p. 23).

Important patterns from your former lives can be used. "Recognition that illness, fears, phobias, personal conflicts and other emphasized conditions of an undesired nature were created in a past lifetime enables the individual to resolve the specific condition" (Cardinal, 1988b, p. 29).

You can use Huichol shamanism, including the Huichol ceremony and sacred dance, "to gain an elevated quality of health, power and harmony through the Huichol 'way of the heart' " (Secunda, 1988, p. 28). Learn to take part in ancient exercises for empowerment and transformation, including the Fire Dance, which awakens the fire energies within to the Tonal, to the world of the animal powers, and the mythical journey to the Nagual, where one's ancestral memories are awakened and where one learns the shaman's way to see and to heal during the *visionary state*" (Viloldo, 1986).

Quartz crystals can be used in healing and in spiritual growth. "Patterns for healing specific diseases, the copper grid system and considerable energy work on elevating the vibration are utilized" (Alper, 1988, p. 27). "This five-day workshop is an in-depth exploration of crystals as a therapeutic tool for healing self and others" (Shinnah, 1988, p. 26).

You can dance with the devas, fly with the fairies, talk with the plants. . . . The oldest way on earth, using common plants/weeds, simple rituals, and compassionate intuition to activate optimum nourishment in all aspects of our being" (Weed, 1988, p. 23).

You can use sound currents: "Electromagnetic healing using sacred sounds is taught. . . . Learn to communicate with nature spirits and work with power animals" (Eagles, 1988, p. 20).

You can use the CHOD healing ceremony of the Tibetan Buddhist lamas. "The CHOD practitioner invites all beings alike, helpers and harmdoers to feast upon his offering, fearlessly cutting both hope and fear, the CHOD practitioner withholds nothing from this offering, not even his own body" (Rinpoche, 1988, p. 13).

The shape of your face and the condition of your skin can be altered by having energy drawn from your head area and then having it put in your right ear by Soviet shamanistic practitioners (Croll-Young, 1987).

Cancer can be prevented or even cured by eating a macrobiotic (all-vegetable) diet (Micho Kushi, cited in Londer, 1985).

You can cure physical ailments and diseases by having a master of qigong come from his hand "and the patient will feel it inside his body. The 'qi' (energy force) moves from my body and has a physical force on the patient" (Yang Baotang, quoted in Gargan, 1986, p. C3).

You can use painted Cherokee Medicine Wheels as personal shields against illness (Mehl, 1986).

You can use Traditional Indian Medicine as "the spiritual focus of the healing process for all people," prevent burnout, and gain "everlasting life" (Monetathchi, 1988, p. 3).

Calligraphy and the art of drawing a smooth and even line, this "indicates that all the joints, muscles and internal organs are in a state of harmonious balance" (Hon, 1985, p. 15).

You can employ Taoist sexual exercises thereby "invigorating and rejuvenating the body's vital functions. Exercises also facilitate the process of linking sexual energy and transcendent states of consciousness" (Chia & Chia, 1987, p. 65).

In Bali, sorcerers and witches who cause you maladies and troubles can be banished by using Balian Taksu, "mediums who convene—while in a trance—with the gods, ancestors and spirits in search of magical or supernatural causes. They and the Balian Osada represent the core of the Balinese healing tradition" (Carpenter, 1986, p. 12).

Exorcism and devil worship overcome physical and mental illness (Bartlett, 1985; Franklyn, 1973; Laurence, 1974; LaVey, 1972; Peck, 1983).

Obviously, these mystical, magical remedies for all ills—even including AIDS—do not work for the reasons specified. When they appear to work at all (which, apparently, is seldom), they most likely do so because people *believe* in them, and not because they have any intrinsic merit. Moreoever, they often do great harm by giving false hope to sufferers, inducing them not to take advantage of regular medical care, and encouraging afflicted individuals to avoid medication, exercise, proper diet, and other measures that would often help them (Savan, 1986; Stalker & Glymour, 1985).

In addition, many devout religionists and transpersonalists who piously believe in God-given or mystical cures, refuse to take their young children for proper medical care, resulting in many unnecessary deaths or the exacerbation of disease. Transpersonal groups keep fighting to permit this kind of child abuse to occur: "At least 43 states—including Massachusetts, California, and Florida—have laws specifically protecting Christian Science parents and others who use an organized form of spiritual healing from child-abuse charges when they fail to seek medical treatment. The Christian Science church has lobbied so successfully that . . . the number of states with such laws grows every year" (Lewin, 1988, p. E16). Christian Science "healing therapy" is also qualified for third-party reimbursement as legitimate treatment.

An example of faith-healing's efforts to stop people from taking advantage of the healing potential of traditionally accepted medical practices, can be found in the case of Ruth Carter Stapleton who died of cancer at the age of fifty-four after "she said she would forgo medical treatment and rely on God to help her." She said that she would use prayer, meditation, and exercise instead (Saxon, 1983, p. 32). Similarly, Beverly Galyeon "was told she had a large malignant breast tumor and that if she had immediate surgery, chemotherapy and radiation, she might be able to live another five to ten years," but she refused to do so and died a year later at the age of forty (Breutsch, 1984, p. 24; Battung, 1984). Refusal of medical interventions is also common in devout religious groups such as the Jehovah's Witnesses. We of course are not arguing against the right of adults to refuse treatment, but against fanatical religious groups that practically force their adherents to refuse it.

More natural means of health maintenance are increasingly being used, especially in the United States. Americans are also becoming more health conscious. However, this is not to say that we are abandoning the medical profession or necessarily becoming obsessed with physical fitness. Although, as stated earlier, one can rationally become vitally absorbed in getting into shape, RET does not endorse a fanatical or obsessive/compulsive absorption.

Pursuit of better health should preferably be a priority for everyone. However, the frenetic, dogmatic, and rigid pursuit of anything is likely to lead to stress, to physical and emotional disorder, and to diminishing returns. This is what often happens in the transpersonal quest for "holistic health."

LACK OF SYSTEMS THEORY AND INTERACTIONISM

Interactionism and systems-oriented theory and techniques have become increasingly popular in psychology and social work. Rational-emotive therapy, somewhat like systems theory, subscribes to interactionism and to what Albert Bandura (1977) calls reciprocal determinism (Ellis, 1958, 1962, 1984a, 1984b, 1984e, 1985, 1986c, 1987b, 1987e, 1988, 1989; Ellis & Dryden, 1987). Transpersonal psychology, on the other hand, often takes interactionism to extremes.

Interactionism implies that cognitions, emotions, and behaviors significantly overlap and interact with and affect each other. Therefore, if we change any of these processes we tend to modify the other two. Also, biological and environmental factors reciprocally interact. In this kind of interactionism, thought, feeling, and action continually influence each other and are never completely disparate.

Transpersonal psychotherapy, as stated above, goes to implausible extremes in its interactionistic stance by positing the absolute unity of all things, including human thoughts, feelings, and actions (Capra, 1983; Deikman, 1982; Houston, 1982; Watts, 1982; Wilber, 1982a, 1982c). However, at the same time, transpersonalism often contradicts itself by asserting that *pure* thought, *pure* emotion, and *pure* intuition exist. Similarly, transpersonalists argue, when we experience these "purities," we humans also acquire "higher" states of consciousness and being. When transpersonal psychologists use many psychotherapeutic methods, including some aspects of RET, they contradict their own theory (Wilber, 1982c).

16

The Dangers of Transpersonalism
A Reply to Ken Wilber's Criticisms

In a recent article titled "Let's Nuke the Transpersonalists," Ken Wilber (in press), one of the leaders of the modern transpersonal movement, objects to an article of mine (A.E.), "Fanaticism That May Lead to a Nuclear Holocaust," in which I briefly pointed out some of the dangers of transpersonalism that are covered in this book (Ellis, 1986a). Because Wilber is so prominent a transpersonalist, let me briefly reply to his objections.

1. Wilber notes that in my article I do not cite books and articles by "respected writers in the field." True. I did not do so because of space limitations in the article. But Wilber may be surprised to see how many "respected writers in the field" I cite in this present book.

2. Wilber accuses me of being a logical positivist, and grandly rips up logical positivism. I was once close to logical positivism, but since 1976 have followed Karl Popper (1985) and W. W. Bartley (1962), who uphold critical rationalism (or critical realism), which holds that scientific theories are to be stated

so that they are falsifiable—as the theory of logical positivism is not stated.

3. Wilber emotionally accuses me of scientism. I am opposed to scientism—and to all kinds of dogmatic *isms* (Ellis, 1962). As Wilber admits, believers in scientism and absolutism "tend to be fanatics." I am glad that he endorses this main point of my criticized article!

4. Wilber wrongly quotes me as saying that "We must incorporate therapeutic teachings and bring them to all the masses." Using rational-emotive psychology, I said *had better,* not *must. Bringing* antimusturbatory teachings to the masses is *not* utopian, as Wilber claims, though *convincing* all of them certainly may be! And I, of course, would not *force* the world's population to learn RET—only encourage them!

5. I do not "approach religion as if it were a disease . . . to be cured at all costs." Instead, I oppose religio*sity,* which I have defined as a dogmatic, fanatical belief in theological religion (e.g., Christianity) *and* in secular religion (e.g., fascism and freudianism) (Ellis, 1982, 1985).

6. Wilber denies that mysticism has dogma or formalism that claims to be the best and only way to describe reality. *Some* mystics, such as Buddha and Wilber, are of course open-minded. But how about St. Augustine, John of the Cross, Joseph Smith, H. P. Blavatsky, Emanuel Swedenborg, the Fox sisters, Maharishi Mahesh Yogi, Jim Jones, Sri Swami Rama, etc.?

7. Virtually all mystics, as Wilber notes, believe in an "absolute spirit," and, as he also states, "believers in absolute systems tend to be fanatics." Again, he endorses one of my main points of view!

8. Wilber claims that mystics "call Spirit many who is really one and that therefore they are tolerant of diverse religious beliefs." But if you firmly believe that there is only One Truth, One God, and One Spirit, you can easily fight, censor, and persecute any group that holds pluralistic or different views. Many mystical cults are combative!

9. Wilber contends that when asked what absolute reality is, mystics respond with silence. What mystics? Not St. Augustine! Not Madame Blavatsky! Not Khomeini!

10. Wilber says that mysticism is undogmatic because "it relies for its validation on direct experience." But direct *personal* experience unbacked by *other* more objective experimentation *is* unfalsifiable and dogmatic! Science, contrary to Wilber's allegation, does *not* rely on personal direct experience but on *repeated* observations. The "direct experience" of mystics includes highly biased, dogmatic *interpretations* and *conclusions* that are usually vague and nondisputable.

11. Wilber notes that "zealots and fanatics come in all flavors (Nazi doctors, for example) just as there are religious fanatics." Right. *Secular* religionists, as I pointed out previously (Ellis, 1982) *can* easily be fanatical and terroristic. But I hypothesize that whereas relatively few scientists are fanatics (and have strong *religiosity* when they are), a much higher proportion of mystics are dogmatists and zealots; and that zealotry tends to be a concomitant of profound mysticism and pious religiousness. I would also guess that zealots and bigots tend to be significantly more mystical and religious than do liberals and democrats.

   This hypothesis, of course, merits empirical study. But, as I note below, such study had better be carefully done.

12. Wilber cites many leading philosophers, psychologists, and scientists who are mystical. True. But I could easily cite some outstanding people, including scientists, who piously believe in astrology, tarot card reading, clairvoyance, psychokinesis, ghosts, reincarnation, UFOs, astral projection, psychic surgery, exorcism, gurus with godly powers, and other "psychic" phenomena.

13. I still would uphold the view, which Wilber quotes me on, that even the greatest thinkers and psychologists who hold transpersonal or transcendental ideas not *necessarily* but very *often* "promulgate almost exactly the kind of absolutistic ideology that is devoutly held by the religious and political sectarians who may some day atomically annihilate the whole human race." Many of them *do* hold this ideology that encourages the sectarians to think in the confused, absolutistic way that they think—and act! Wilber keeps pointing out that not *all* transpersonalists are devout, absolutistic, or violent. Of course they aren't. But my point is that if we thoroughly examined a thousand transpersonalists and another thousand nontranspersonalists, a significantly higher percentage of the former than the latter would be found to be dogmatic, bigoted, and violence prone.

   Before such a study is actually done, however, let me warn that many transpersonalists who answer any questionnaire about their dogmatism and hostility will very probably *claim* to be openminded and tolerant—just as many religious people *claim* to be happily married when it is dubious that they actually are. So let the researchers beware!

14. Wilber claims that morality is based on human sameness. We do good for others because we realize, with Schopenhauer, "that we all share the same transcendental self or consciousness." This is drivel, since the human sameness on which

morality is often based is a very down-to-earth, observable human sameness and has nothing to do with the transcendental or superhuman concept of self or commonality.

15. Wilber points out that most Eastern followers of reincarnation and karma "don't even like to kill insects, let alone people." He forgets that *some* of these followers devoutly believe that they will be rewarded in their afterlife, if they *do* kill the disbelievers and "heathens" in this life—and that they will be severely punished if they don't!

16. Wilber states that I give "four suppositions that are supposed to define the entire field" of transpersonalism. For brevity's sake, after the editor had cut down my originally longer paper, I mentioned these four concepts in my article, but I include no less than 35 basic transpersonal ideologies in the present book on the dangers of transpersonalism. And I do not believe that *all* transpersonalists subscribe to these concepts, but as far as I can see virtually all of them subscribe to many of these ideas.

17. Wilber: Ellis "cannot give so much as a single case of a person describing himself or herself as a transpersonal psychologist who has ever engaged in terrorist or similarly grave antisocial activity." In this present book on the dangers of transpersonal psychology, I cite many instances where transpersonalists definitely did resort to terrorism and to similarly grave antisocial activity (see chapter 8).

18. Wilber quotes a few transpersonalists who do not strictly go along with my statement that "absolute reality exists, and when we find the true doctrine that reveals it, we reach absolute, invariant, unchangeable, ineffable truth." But he fails to note that innumerable transpersonalists do subscribe to this view, or something close to it.

19. Wilber states: "I don't know anybody who thinks that reincarnation has been empirically proven." Well, his contacts are strictly limited! I personally know and have heard of many believers in reincarnation—e.g., Shirley MacLaine!—who are positive that they and other people have talked to dead "spirits." Although Ian Stevenson was agnostic about the issue of reincarnation, hundreds of other investigators have been quite convinced of its "empirical" existence.

20. Wilber takes me to task for saying that transcendentalists believe that "all living and inanimate things merge into one fundamental unit." But he merely shows that *he* takes issue with my word *merge*. Many mystics *do* see all things as merging into one unit. Thus, Deikman (1972, p. 1), a mystical-minded psychiatrist, says that mystics believe that "the awareness of a tree is not different from our own, it is continuous with it and awareness is the origin of the entire system." And Taoism, the world's most popular form of mysticism, definitely holds that inanimate matter and animate life are one, and essentially merge.

21. Wilber: "Most transpersonalists are extremely sympathetic to science, and wish that the spirit of scientific enterprise—a certain honesty, integrity, and openness in research—be used as much as possible." No, transpersonalists often give lip-service to science and use scientific findings (as Fritjof Capra does) to illegitimately bolster their mystical beliefs. But *Webster's New World Dictionary* defines *mystic* as "of obscure or occult character or meaning" and "beyond human comprehension." And it defines *transcendental* as "based on a search for reality through spiritual intuition." Surely this is not science! Modern philosophies of science, moreover, while abjuring logical positivism, hold that to be "scientific" a hypothesis had better be falsifiable. As far as I know, none of the truly transpersonal theories are falsifiable.

21. Wilber says that I do not understand the crucial difference between regressive prerational states (which presumably include the dangers I have accused transpersonal believers of fomenting) and "higher development *trans*-rational states." No, I don't quite understand this difference, though I have read his well-written paper on "the pre-trans fallacy" (Wilber, 1982c). As far as I can see, both states are equally mystical, magical, and transpersonal. But even if Wilber is right, he himself (in his pre-trans fallacy paper) accuses many transpersonalists of adhering to the pre-trans fallacy, so that he substantiates the major point of my criticized paper. For I did not say that *all* transpersonalists are dangerous but that a *great many* are. Apparently, Wilber agrees!

As can be seen, I hope, from the above comments, Wilber's critique of my critique has much heat and little light. Exactly what I would expect of most transpersonal thinkers!

17

Summary and Conclusions

The purpose of this book is to demonstrate that transpersonal psychology and psychotherapy (TP) propose to be humanistic and therapeutic but fall quite short in these respects. None of the modern therapies are foolproof, and there is even some evidence that the conventional ones, such as psychoanalysis, often do harm.

The material presented here suggests the likelihood that TP does much more harm and much less good than the psychotherapies that are regularly used today. Some of its most harmful aspects are these:

1. It fosters absolutistic and dogmatic thinking, just the kind of cognition that is the core of much emotional and behavioral disturbance.

2. It encourages devout allegiance to, and often worship of, leaders and gurus and thereby abets neurotic dependency.

3. It tends to be perfectionistic and to promise its followers absolute success, perfect performance, universal love, and unalloyed bliss. None of these promises are likely to be fulfilled in the real world.

4. It discourages innumerable disturbed people from receiving more beneficial forms of psychological, psychiatric, and medical treatment that might well offer them real help with their problems.

5. It often promulgates the notion that mere devout belief in some higher power, guru, or transcendental philosophy will miraculously cure its followers of mental and physical ills. It thereby discourages them from using methods of therapy that require hard work and practice and that have some degree of proven efficiency.

6. It often uses emotive appeals and techniques that are either too passive and unforceful or that are frenetic, hysterical, and even disturbance producing.

7. It frequently promises certainty and thereby leads its followers into disillusionment when such certainty cannot actually be achieved.

8. In many instances, it literally promises miracles that are most unlikely to be fulfilled.

9. It frequently insists on people being ruled by unchangeable karma or fate and thereby discourages them from actively directing their own lives.

10. It gives many people the grandiose idea that they are god or have a god within, and that therefore they can accomplish practically anything.

11. It sponsors many rigid, compulsive rituals and ceremonies that detract from spontaneous living and from human freedom.

12. It encourages an enormous amount of lying, trickery, and cheating of millions of gullible individuals who fervently wish,

against all evidence, to believe in mediums, fortune-tellers, faith-healers, and other "psychics."

13. It promotes authoritarian cults, with leaders who are to be followed blindly, and who often persuasively or forcefully deprive their followers of human rights and freedom.

14. It sometimes encourages satanism, devil worship, and sadistic rituals.

15. It frequently espouses the concept of Nirvana or desirelessness, thereby sabotaging human drive, productivity, creativity, and achievement.

16. It often makes sacred and deifies the normal experiences of birth and death.

17. Many devout religious and transpersonal sects believe that because they know Absolute Truth and the Perfect Right Way, they are entirely justified in inflicting war, terrorism, torture, and other kinds of violence and death on any and all who do not believe in their creeds.

18. Transpersonal psychology discourages people from accepting themselves fully and unconditionally, just because they are human and alive, but encourages them to accept themselves only very conditionally, according to the precepts of various TP sects.

19. It often disavows human happiness and sponsors many ascetic ideas and observances.

20. It frequently overemphasizes social conformity and/or pushes people to so dedicate themselves to "spiritual" tasks that they neglect or sabotage social interest and cooperation.

21. It often stoutly refuses to face or accept grim reality and thereby sabotages efforts to change it.

22. It blocks some of the main goals and ideals of humanism by its obsessive interest in superhuman, magical, and godly pathways.

23. It often tries inconsistently and hypocritically to get people to be "egoless" by *choosing* to be and to be "desireless" by *desiring* to be!

24. It tends to devoutly uphold reincarnation and to endorse striving for it in many ritualistic and ascetic ways that sabotage human happiness in the one life we can be sure of having.

25. It strongly favors fanatical holistic medicine and faith-healing, opposes conventional medical treatment, and thereby probably helps kill or maim many more people than it truly "saves."

26. It hypocritically uses scientific theories (such as the Heisenberg principle of indeterminacy) and tools (such as biofeedback machines) to "substantiate" its transcendental, suprahuman claims.

27. By emphasizing reliance on personal, intuitive experience, as well as reliance on sacred "truths" and "holy" leaders, transpersonalism discourages people from obtaining insight into themselves and their self-defeating behaviors and from making concerted efforts to use these insights to change themselves.

28. Transpersonal psychology often encourages and bolsters neurotic defenses by helping people ignore and refuse to accept grim reality and to adopt idealistic, utopian views.

29. It ignores most of the main findings and practices of behavioral therapy and takes some behavioral practices (such as dieting and exercise) to harmful extremes.

30. It often deifies the expression of feeling and thereby trains people to be angrier, whinier, and more depressed than they would otherwise be.

31. It frequently limits and blocks interpersonal relationships by restricting them to members of a cult and/or by pushing them to relate automatically to themselves, to "Higher Powers," or to the inanimate universe.

32. Transpersonal psychology and psychotherapy often objects to the scientific testing and evaluation of therapy techniques and instead relies on anecdotal endorsements that are highly questionable and that are frequently faked.

We do not claim that transpersonal psychotherapy is of no value whatsoever and never helps people with their emotional problems. Many kinds of therapy, some of them quite bizarre, sometimes help. For all its limitations, TP may include these advantages: (1) It gives people hope that they *can* change themselves if they change some of their self-defeating philosophies. (2) It sometimes motivates people to act differently and thereby to do something to change themselves. (3) Its compulsive rituals and asceticism may help some individuals reduce their low frustration tolerance. (4) It sometimes includes some humanistic and peace-oriented teachings along with its bigotries and warlike views. (5) It questions scientism and one-sided materialism and encourages a peculiar kind of "openmindedness." (6) It opposes some inefficient therapies such as classical psychoanalysis and orthodox behavior therapy.

In spite of these advantages, transpersonal psychology and psychotherapy do great harm and present enormous dangers. We do not, of course, advocate that they thereby be censored or abolished—such advocacy would put us in their own absolutistic, bigoted camp! We hope, however, that scientists and humanists will keep vigorously investigating psychic and spiritual "phenomena" and will incisively demonstrate when it is dubious, faked, and invalid and when it leads to harmful illusion.

References

Included in the following list of references are a good many items on rational-emotive therapy (RET), many of which are published or distributed by the Institute for Rational-Emotive Therapy, 45 East 65th Street, New York, NY 10021-6593, or available by calling (212) 535-0822. The Institute will continue to make available these and other materials on rational-emotive therapy, as well as to present talks, seminars, workshops, and other presentations in the area of human growth and rational living. Interested individuals can send for its current catalogue of publications, events, recordings, and other materials.

Abbas, S. S. 1986. Psychotherapeutic services in urban areas of Pakistan. *International Psychologist* 27(2):16.

———. 1986. *Psychotherapeutic services in urban areas of Pakistan.* Islamabad, Pakistan: National Institute of Psychology.

Adler, A. 1964. *Social interest: A challenge of mankind.* New York: Capricorn.

Agena, K. 1983. The return of enchantment. *New York Times Magazine* (November 27): 66–80.

Ajami, F. 1986. *The vanished Imam.* Ithaca, N.Y.: Cornell University Press.

Ajaya, S. 1984. *Psychotherapy: East and West.* Honnendale, Pa.: Himalayan International Institute of Yoga Science and Philosophy.

All Together Now: Meditate. 1985. *New York Times* (October 16):
A24.

Alper, F. 1988. Generating crystal power. *Joy Lake Mountain Center
Catalogue of Events,* 27.

Amitabh, S. P. 1982. The Rajneesh Ashram. *Journal of Humanistic
Psychology* 22:19-42.

Amritu, S. D. 1982. Original face. *Bhagwan,* no. 1:16-25.

Anthony, D., Ecker, B., and Wilber, K., eds. 1987. *Spiritual choices:
The problem of recognizing authentic paths of inner transformation.* New York: Paragon House.

Anti-Abortion Activist Says Clinic Bombers May Be Right. 1985.
Church and State 38:136.

Anti-Abortion Campaign Escalates to Holy War. 1986. *Church and
State* 39(6):17-18.

Apple, R. W., Jr. 1985. 329 Lost on Air-India plane after crash near
Ireland; bomb is suspected as cause. *New York Times* (June 24):
A1, A10.

Applebaum, S. A. 1979. *Out in inner space: A psychoanalyst explores
the new therapies.* New York: Anchor Press/Doubleday.

Aronson, E. 1976. *The social animal.* San Francisco: W. H. Freeman.

Asimov, I. 1984. Is big brother watching? *The Humanist* 44(4):6-
10.

Baker, J. R. 1986. Fundamentalism as anti-intellectualism. *The Humanist* 46 (2): 26-28.

Bales, J. 1988. Fundamentalist clients: Overcoming suspicion. *APA
Monitor* (June): 20.

Bandura, A. 1977. *Social learning theory.* Englewood Cliffs, N.J.:
Prentice-Hall.

Bard, J. 1980. *Rational-emotive therapy in practice.* Champaign, Ill.:
Research Press.

———. 1987. *I don't like asparagus.* Cleveland, Ohio: Psychology
Department, Cleveland State University.

Barnhart, J. E. 1986. On the relative sincerity of faith-healers. *Free Inquiry,* 6(2): 24–29.

Baron, J. 1985. *Rationality and intelligence.* New York: Cambridge University Press.

Barron, J. 1987. Dancing at dawn in rite of cosmic harmony. *New York Times* (August 17): A1, B3.

Bartlett, K. 1985. Writer on exorcisms still talking about things most people shun. *Tucson Arizonian* (December): 3.

Bartley, W. W. 1962. *The retreat to commitment.* New York: Knopf.

Battung, D. 1984. Dream weaver. *Association for Humanistic Psychology Newsletter* (April): 25.

Beck, A. T. 1976. *Cognitive therapy and the emotional disorders.* New York: New American Library.

Beck, A. T., Rush, A. J., Shaw, B. F., and Emery, G. 1979. *Cognitive therapy of depression.* New York: Guilford Press.

Bellack, A. S., and Hersen, M., eds. 1985. *Dictionary of behavior therapy techniques.* New York: Pergamon.

Benderly, B. L. 1988. Prophet and losses. *Psychology Today* 22(2): 68, 74.

Bennett, D. 1986. After death: Noetic scientists poke at edges of the beyond. *APA Monitor* 17(2): 13.

Benson, H., with Proctor, W. 1984. *Beyond the relaxation response.* New York: Times Books.

Bering–Jensen, H. 1986. The search for a solution to a historical quagmire. *Insight* 2(4): 26–29.

Bernard, M. E. 1986. *Staying alive in an irrational world: Albert Ellis and rational–emotive therapy.* South Melbourne, Australia: Carlson/Macmillan.

Bernard, M. E., and DiGiuseppe, R., eds. 1988. *Inside rational-emotive therapy.* Orlando, Fla.: Academic Press.

Bernstein, R. 1986. Five dead, 50 hurt as bomb is hurled on a Paris street. *New York Times* (September 18): A1, A11.

Beware of Your Visions, Even Angels. 1987. *Insight* (October): 50–52.

Bhatty, M. 1983. Iskon (International Society for Krishna Consciousness) mimics Christian propagandists. *American Atheist* 25(3): 22–24.

———. 1984a. I am god! *American Atheist* 26(7): 37–38.

———. 1984b. Women and the law of karma. *American Atheist* 26(8): 37–38.

———. 1985. Digitizing destiny. *American Atheist* 27(5): 28–29.

———. 1987. Psychic shenanigans? *American Atheist* 29(6): 43–44.

Bible Is Cited to Defend Beatings at Church School. 1984. *New York Times* (June 2): 36.

Biela, A., and Tobacyk, J. J. 1987. Self-transcendence in the Agoral Gathering. *Journal of Humanistic Psychology* 27(4): 390–405.

Bishop, K. 1986, Jury being picked in retrial of Guyana cultist. *New York Times* (September 21): A27.

Blackmore, S. 1987. The elusive open mind: Ten years of negative research in parapsychology. *The Skeptical Inquirer* 11(3): 244–255.

Booth, J. 1986. *Psychic paradoxes.* Buffalo, N.Y.: Prometheus Books.

Bordewich, F. M. 1988. *New York Times Magazine* (May 1): 37–44.

Bourne, E. 1986. In defense of transpersonal psychology. *APA Monitor* 17(7): 2.

Boyd, G. M. 1988, Regan book depicts president steered by wife and the stars. *New York Times* (May 9): A1, B7.

Branden, N. 1984. *The psychology of self-esteem.* New York: Bantam; 2nd ed., Los Angeles: Tarcher.

Braude, S. E. 1986. *The limits of influence: Psychokinesis and the philosophy of science.* London: Routledge & Kegan Paul.

Breutsch, A. 1984. Tribute to a friend. *Association for Humanistic Psychology Newsletter* (April): 24.

Bridgewater, J. 1984. Acceptance of the occult. *Psychology Today* (April): 50.

Briggs, K. A. 1984a. British Center monitors Soviet attacks on religion. *New York Times* (July 22): 4.

———. 1984b. Sixteen Jewish groups protest to Israel. *New York Times* (August 14): A11.

Brilliant, M. 1984. Shamir asserts bus plot arrests foiled disaster. *New York Times* (August 30): A1, A4.

Brink, A. 1984. Bertrand Russell's conversion of 1901 or the benefits of creative illness. *Russell* 4(1): 83–99.

Brooks, A. 1986. "Cults" and the aged: A new family issue. *New York Times* (April 26): 52.

Brown, E. A. 1984. Intuition and inner guidance. *Association for Humanistic Psychology Newsletter* (May): 18.

Bufe, C. 1987. *Astrology: Fraud or superstition?* San Francisco: See Sharp Press.

Bugental, J. F. T. 1971. The search for the hidden God. *Voices* 7(1): 33–37.

Busch, R. 1987. The unmasking of psychic Jason Michaels. *The Skeptical Inquirer* 9(4): 327–330.

Butterfield, F. 1984. Sect members assert they are misunderstood. *New York Times* (June 24): 16.

Caddy, P. 1984a. A course in miracles weekend. *Gathering of the Ways Catalogue,* 11.

———. 1984b. Experience the power of Mount Shasta. *Gathering of the Ways Catalogue,* 4.

Calderon, E., Cowan, R., Sharon, D., and Sharon, F. K. 1982. *The words of a Peruvian healer.* New York: North Atlantic Books.

Campbell, C. 1984. Moslem students in U.S. rediscovering Islam. *New York Times* (May 13): 1, 4.

Cannon, S. 1982. Caveat emptor. *Association for Humanistic Psychology Newsletter* (November 1): 15.

Capra, F. 1983. *The Tao of physics.* Boulder, Colo.: Shambhala.

Cardinal, M. 1986a. Mastering the seventh-sense soul level. *Joy Lake Mountain Seminar Catalogue,* 28.

———. 1986b. ESP: Extended sensory perception is a natural function for everyone. *Joy Lake Mountain Seminar Catalogue,* 23.

———. 1988a. Reincarnation: Examination of the cyclic rebirth theory and memo therapy exercises for past life recall. *Joy Lake Mountain Seminar Catalogue,* 15.

———. 1988b. Examining the theory of reincarnation experience past life recall through memo-therapy. *Joy Lake Mountain Center Catalogue of Events,* 29.

Carpenter, B. 1986. Healing in Bali. *Association for Humanistic Psychology Perspective,* (March): 12–13.

Castaneda, C. 1968. *The teachings of Don Juan.* New York: Simon & Schuster.

———. 1984. *The fire from within.* New York: Simon & Schuster.

Chase, M. 1988. From umpires, a get-tough call on Martin. *New York Times* (June 4): 1, 25.

Chaudhuri, H. 1975. The meeting of East and West. *Synthesis* 1(2): 20–40.

Chia, M., and Chia, M. 1987. Taoist secrets of love. *East West* (January): 65–68.

A Chinese garden of sanity. 1976. Mt. Vernon, N.Y.: Peter Pauper.

Church of Scientology Is Sued for $1 Billion. 1984. *New York Times* (January 2): D14.

Clarke, R. O. 1988. The narcissistic guru: A profile of Bhagwan Shree Rajneesh. *Free Inquiry* 8(2): 33–45.

Clendinen, D. 1984a. Two views at odds on Vermont sect. *New York Times* (June 20): 5.

———. 1984b. Child beatings question of abuse or discipline. *New York Times* (July·1): 14.

Clines, F. X. 1986. The I.R.A. is pointing its rifle at the working man. *New York Times* (August 17): E3.

Cohn, R. C. 1983. Particle/waves—what do they mean for psychology and religion? *Voices* 19(2): 69–75.

Colby, W. E. 1984. Taking steps to contain terrorism. *New York Times* (July 8): E21.

Collins, B. 1986. In defense of transpersonal psychology. *APA Monitor* 17(7): 2.

Colodzin, B. 1983. Body dynamics: An overview. *Association for Humanistic Psychology Newsletter* (July): 16–19.

Conn, J. H. 1988. Hypnosis and reincarnation. *Society of Clinical and Experimental Hypnosis Newsletter* 29(1): 2.

Corey, G. 1986a. *Case approach to counseling and psychotherapy.* Monterey, Calif.: Brooks/Cole.

———. 1986b. *Theory and practice of counseling and psychotherapy,* 3rd ed. Monterey, Calif.: Brooks/Cole.

Cowan, T. M. 1973. State-specific sciences. *Science* 180: 1005.

Crawford, T. (speaker). 1982. Workshop on rational-emotive therapy and communication (October): Los Angeles.

Croll-Young, C. 1987. Meeting with Soviet healers. *Associaton for Humanistic Psychology Perspective* (August): 7.

Crossette, B. 1986. A corner of Malaysia is rocked by political rage. *New York Times* (March 21): A2.

Crouch, S. 1985. Nationalism of fools: Farrakhan brings it all back home. *Village Voice* (October 29): 21–23, 102.

Culver, R. B., and Ianna, P. A. 1984. *The Gemini syndrome: A scientific evaluation of astrology.* Buffalo, N.Y.: Prometheus Books.

Dart, J. 1984. Exorcism on the rise. *Washington Post News Service* (January 8): 3.

Davis, R. G. 1984. Oberammergau play: Deeply rooted offense. *New York Times* (June 3): 21.

Dean, G. 1987. Does astrology need to be true? Part 2: The answer is No. *The Skeptical Inquirer* 11(3): 257.

Deikman, A. 1972. The meaning of everything. *Association for Humanistic Psychology Newsletter* (April): 14.

———. 1982. *The Observing self: Mysticism and psychotherapy.* Boston: Beacon Press.

deMille, R. 1976. *Castaneda's journey: The power and the allegory.* Santa Barbara, Calif.: Capra Press.

———. 1980. *The Don Juan papers: Further Castaneda controversies.* Santa Barbara, Calif.: Ross-Erickson.

———. 1981. Review of *The wave of the shaman* by Michael Harner. *Association for Humanistic Psychology Newsletter* (August): 25.

Dennett, M. K. 1985. Firewalking: Reality or illusion? *The Skeptical Inquirer* 10(1): 36–41.

DiGiuseppe, R. 1986. The implications of the philosophy of science for rational–emotive theory and psychotherapy. *Psychotherapy* 23: 634–39.

Dowlatashahi, H. 1983. *Seven essays on unity.* London: New Universal Union.

Drack, J. 1982. Review of *Mind of our mother* by B. Samples. *Association for Humanistic Psychology Newsletter* (November): 21.

Dryden, W. 1984. *Rational-emotive therapy: Fundamentals and innovations.* London: Croom Helm.

Eagles, N. K. 1988. Sound current. *Joy Lake Mountain Center Catalogue of Events,* 20.

Edwards, P. 1987. The case against reincarnation. *Free Inquiry* 7(3): 46–53.

Ehrlich, M. 1986. Taoism and psychotherapy. *Journal of Contemporary Psychology* 16(1): 23–38.

Elk, W. B. The wisdom of Lakota Shamanism. *Joy Lake Mountain Center Catalogue of Events,* 12.

Ellis, A. 1954. *The American sexual tragedy.* New York: Twayne. Rev. ed., 1962. New York: Lyle Stuart and Grove Press.

Ellis, A. 1956. The effectiveness of psychotherapy with individuals who have severe homosexual problems. *Journal of Consulting Psychology* 20: 191–195.

———. 1957. *How to live with a "neurotic."* New York: Crown. Rev. ed., 1975. North Hollywood, Calif.: Wilshire Books.

———. 1958. Rational psychotherapy. *Journal of General Psychology* 59: 245–253.

———. 1962. *Reason and emotion in psychotherapy.* Secaucus, N.J.: Lyle Stuart and Citadel Press.

———. 1963. *The Intelligent woman's guide to manhunting.* New York: Lyle Stuart and Dell.

———. 1965. *Suppressed: Seven key essays publishers dared not print.* Chicago: New Classics House.

———. 1969a. A cognitive approach to behavior therapy. *International Journal of Psychiatry* 8: 896–900.

———. 1969b. A weekend of rational encounter. *Encounter,* edited by A. Burton, 112–127. San Francisco: Jossey-Bass.

———. 1971. *Growth through reason.* North Hollywood, Calif.: Willshire Books.

———. (speaker). 1972a. *How to stubbornly refuse to be ashamed of anything.* Cassette recording. New York: Institute for Rational-Emotive Therapy.

———. 1972b. *Psychotherapy and the value of a human being.* New York: Institute for Rational-Emotive Therapy.

———. 1972c. What does transpersonal psychology have to offer the art and science of psychotherapy? *Voices* 8(3): 10–20. Revised version, 1973. *Rational Living* 8(1): 20–28.

———. 1973a. *Humanistic psychotherapy: The rational-emotive approach.* New York: McGraw-Hill.

———. 1973b. Is transpersonal psychology humanistic? *Association for Humanistic Psychology Newsletter* (May-June): 10–13.

———. 1975a. Comments on Frank's "The limits of humanism." *The Humanist* 35(5): 43–45.

Ellis, A. (speaker). 1975b. *RET and assertiveness training.* Cassette recording. New York: Institute for Rational-Emotive Therapy.

————. 1976a. The biological basis of human irrationality. *Journal of Individual Psychology* 32: 145–168. Reprinted. New York: Institute for Rational-Emotive Therapy.

————. (speaker). 1976b. *Solving emotional problems.* Cassette recording. New York: Institute for Rational-Emotive Therapy.

————. 1976c. *Sex and the liberated man.* Secaucus, N.J.: Lyle Stuart.

————. (speaker). 1976d. *Conquering low frustration tolerance.* Cassette recording. New York: Institute for Rational-Emotive Therapy.

————. 1977a. *Anger—how to live with and without it.* Secaucus, N.J.: Citadel Press.

————. 1977b. Fun as psychotherapy. *Rational Living* 12(1): 2–6. Also on cassette recording. New York: Institute for Rational-Emotive Therapy.

————. (speaker). 1977c. *A garland of rational songs.* Songbook and cassette recording. New York: Institute for Rational-Emotive Therapy.

————. 1977d. Religious belief in the United States today. *The Humanist* 37(2): 38–41.

————. 1977e. Why "scientific" professionals believe mystical nonsense. *Psychiatric Opinion* 14(2): 27–30.

————. (speaker). 1977f. *Conquering the dire need for love.* Cassette recording. New York: Institute for Rational-Emotive Therapy.

————. 1978. *I'd like to stop but . . . Dealing with addictions.* Cassette recording. New York: Institute for Rational-Emotive Therapy.

————. 1979a. Discomfort anxiety: A new cognitive behavioral construct. Part 1. *Rational Living* 14(2): 3–8.

————. 1979b. The issue of force and energy in behavioral change. *Journal of Contemporary Psychotherapy* 10: 83–97.

————. 1979c. Rational-emotive therapy: Research data that support the clinical and personality hypotheses of RET and other modes of cognitive-behavior therapy. In *Theoretical and empirical foun-*

dations of rational-emotive therapy, edited by A. Ellis and J. M. Whiteley, 101–173. Monterey, Calif.: Brooks/Cole.

Ellis, A. 1979d. *The intelligent woman's guide to dating and mating.* Secaucus, N.J.: Lyle Stuart.

———. 1980a. Discomfort anxiety: A new cognitive behavioral construct. Part 2. *Rational Living* 15(1): 25–30.

———. 1980b. Psychotherapy and atheistic values. A response to A. E. Bergin's "Psychotherapy and religious values." *Journal of Consulting and Clinical Psychology* 48: 635–639.

———. 1980c. The value of efficiency in psychotherapy. *Psychotherapy.* 17(4): 414–419.

———. 1981a. Rational-emotive group therapy. In *Basic approaches to group psychotherapy and group counseling,* edited by G. M. Gazda, 381–412. Springfield, Ill.: Thomas.

———. 1981b. The rational-emotive approach to thanatology. In *Behavior therapy in terminal care: A humanistic approach,* edited by H. J. Sobel, 151–176. Cambridge, Mass.: Ballinger.

———. 1983a. Self-direction in sport and life. *Rational Living* 17(1): 27–34.

———. 1983b. *The case against religiosity.* New York: Institute for Rational-Emotive Therapy.

———. 1983c. Albert Ellis's opinion. *Newsletter of the American Academy of Psychotherapists* (June/July): 2.

———. 1983d. The philosophic implications and dangers of some popular behavior therapy techniques. In *Perspectives in behavior therapy in the eighties,* edited by M. Rosenbaum, C. M. Franks, and Y. Jaffe, 131–151. New York: Springer.

———. 1984a. The essence of RET—1984. *Journal of Rational-Emotive Therapy* 2(1): 19–25.

———. 1984b. Rational-emotive therapy. In *Current psychotherapies,* edited by R. J. Corsini, 3d ed., 197–238. Itasca, Ill.: Peacock.

Ellis, A. 1984c. Intellectual fascism. *Journal of the Institute for the New Man* 1(1): 39–54. Reprinted. New York: Institute for Rational-Emotive Therapy.

———. 1984d. The place of meditation in cognitive-behavior therapy and rational-emotive therapy. In *Meditation: Classic and contemporary perspectives,* edited by D. H. Shapiro and R. N. Walsh, 671–673. New York: Aldine.

———. 1984e. Is the unified-interaction approach to cognitive-behavior modification a reinvention of the wheel? *Clinical Psychology Review* 4: 215–218.

———. 1985. *Overcoming resistance: Rational-emotive therapy with difficult clients.* New York: Springer.

———. 1986a. Fanaticism that may lead to a nuclear holocaust: The contributions of scientific counseling and psychotherapy. *Journal of Counseling and Development* 65: 146–51.

———. 1986b. Do some religious beliefs help create emotional disturbance? *Psychotherapy in Private Practice* 4(4): 101–106.

———. 1986c. Rational-emotive therapy applied to relationship therapy. *Journal of Rational-Emotive Therapy:* 4–21.

———. 1987a. The evolution of rational-emotive therapy (RET) and cognitive behavior therapy (CBT). In *The evolution of psychotherapy,* edited by J. K. Zeig, 107–133. New York: Brunner/Mazel.

———. 1987b. The impossibility of achieving consistently good mental health. *American Psychologist* 42: 364–375.

———. 1987c. Testament of a humanist. *Free Inquiry* 7(2): 21.

———. 1987d. A sadly neglected cognitive element in depression. *Cognitive Therapy and Research* 11: 121–146.

———. 1987e. Integrative developments in rational-emotive therapy (RET). *Journal of Integrative and Eclectic Psychotherapy* 6: 470–479.

———. 1988. *How to stubbornly refuse to make yourself miserable about anything—yes, anything!* Secaucus, N.J.: Lyle Stuart.

Ellis, A.. 1989. Rational-emotive therapy. In *Current psychotherapies,* edited by R. J. Corsini and D. Wedding, 4th ed. Itasca, Ill.: Peacock.

Ellis, A., and Abrams, E. 1978. *Brief psychotherapy in medical and health practice.* New York: Springer.

Ellis, A., and Becker, I. 1982. *A guide to personal happiness.* North Hollywood, Calif.: Wilshire Books.

Ellis, A., and Bernard, M. E., eds. 1983. *Rational-emotive approaches to problems of childhood.* New York: Plenum.

———. 1985. *Clinical applications of rational-emotive therapy.* New York: Plenum.

Ellis, A., and Dryden, W. 1987. *The practice of rational-emotive therapy.* New York: Springer.

Ellis, A., and Grieger, R., eds. 1986. *Handbook of rational-emotive therapy.* 2 vols. New York: Springer.

Ellis, A., and Harper, R. A. 1961. *A guide to successful marriage.* North Hollywood, Calif.: Wilshire Books.

———. 1975. *A new guide to rational living.* North Hollywood, Calif.: Wilshire Books.

Ellis, A., and Knaus, W. 1977. *Overcoming procrastination.* New York: New American Library.

Ellis, A., McInerney, J. F., DiGiuseppe, R., and Yeager, R. J. 1988. *Rational-emotive therapy with alcoholics and substance abusers.* New York: Pergamon.

Ellis, A., and Whiteley, J. M., eds. 1979. *Theoretical and empirical foundations of rational-emotive therapy.* Monterey, Calif.: Brooks/Cole.

Emery, C. E., Jr. 1987. Catching Geller in the act. *The Skeptical Inquirer* 10: 75–80.

———. 1988. An investigation of psychic crime-busting. *The Skeptical Inquirer* 12: 403–410.

Emery, M. R. 1986. Parapsychology: The psi connection. *Association for Humanistic Psychology Perspective* (February): 8.

Emmett, G. 1973. *A psychoanalyst's journal into expanding consciousness: The Africa experience.* New York: Africa Institute of America.

Epstein, R. 1983. Review of *Play to live* by Alan Watts. *Association for Humanistic Psychology Newsletter* (May): 25.

Fairfield, P. 1984. Workshop on medicine as a spiritual practice. *Gathering of the Ways* (Summer): 7.

A Faith to Shed Inhibitions. 1984. *New York Times* (July 11): A21.

Ferguson, M. 1980. *The Aquarian conspiracy.* Los Angeles: Tarcher.

Fichten, C. 1984 [1983]. Scientist denies astrology breakthrough! *APA Monitor* 15(5): 5.

Fisher, K. 1985. Abuse of therapeutic techniques harms public. *APA Monitor* 16(4): 7, 22–23.

Flasher, B. A monkey speaks out. *Association for Humanistic Psychology Newsletter:* 19–20.

Flew, A. 1986. Parapsychology, miracles, and repeatability. *The Skeptical Inquirer* 10(4): 319–325.

————., ed. 1987. *Readings in the philosophical problems of parapsychology.* Buffalo, N.Y.: Prometheus Books.

Flynn, T. 1986. God helps those who help themselves: The wild world of fundamentalist fund-raising. *Free Inquiry* 6(2): 38–42.

Fontana, D. 1987. Self-assertion and self-negation in Buddhist psychology. *Journal of Humanistic Psychology* 27(2): 175–194.

Ford, F. L. 1985. *Political murder.* Cambridge, Mass.: Harvard University Press.

Forum. 1985. The promise of the Forum, 4. San Francisco: Werner Erhard Associates.

Fowler, G., and Crawford, B. 1988. *Border radio.* Dallas, Tex.: Texas Monthly Press.

Frank, J. 1975. The limits of humanism. *The Humanist* 35(5): 50–52.

Franklyn, J., ed. 1973. *A dictionary of the occult.* New York: Causeway Books.

Frazier, K. 1986. *Science confronts the paranormal.* Buffalo, N.Y.: Prometheus Books.

———. 1987. London newspaper series on Uri Geller reveals long record of deception. *The Skeptical Inquirer* 11(3): 226–228.

Freedman, S. G. 1987. Abortion bombings suspect: A portrait of piety and rage. *New York Times* (May 1): A1, B4.

Free Mind. 1987. Faith in astrology. *Free Mind* (June): 8.

Frick, W. B. 1982. Conceptual foundations of self-actualization. *Journal of Humanistic Psychology* 22(4): 33–52.

Friedman, T. L. 1984a. Lebanese losing identity in a retreat into factions. *New York Times* (May 31): A1, A8.

———. 1984b. Lebanon: The Iranian presence. *New York Times Magazine* (July 12): 34.

———. 1985. Israelis believe pro-Libya group raided airports. *New York Times* (December 30): A1, A8.

Fritz, D. 1984. Creating the ideal birth: The mystery of birth and life in a human body. Summer workshop. *Gathering of the Ways Catalogue,* 8.

Frye, R. M., ed. 1984. *Is God a creationist? The religious case against creation-science.* New York: Scribners.

Fuller, A. C. 1980. Carl Rogers, religion, and the role of psychology in American culture. *Journal of Humanistic Psychology* 22(4): 21–32.

Gardner, M. 1981. Science: Good, bad and bogus. Buffalo, N.Y.: Prometheus Books.

———. 1983. Review of *Frames of meaning* by H. M. Collins and T. J. Pinch. *Free Inquiry* 3(4): 46–47.

———. 1986. *The wreck of the Titanic foretold?* Buffalo, N.Y.: Prometheus Books.

———. 1987–88. Psychic astronomy. *Free Inquiry* (Winter): 26–29.

Gardner, M. 1987. Science-fantasy religious cults. *Free Inquiry* 7(3), 31–35.

Gargan, E. A. 1986. A traditional Chinese therapy harnesses the "vital force." *New York Times* (December 21): 23.

Gibbs, J. C. 1981. The near death experience: Balancing Siegel's view. *American Psychologist* 36: 1457–1458.

Goldberg, S. 1988. No reason to believe that astrology is true. *New York Times* (May 29): E16.

Goleman, D. 1979. Good grief! Gurdjieff! *Psychology Today* 34(4): 16, 92.

———. 1985. In the spirit of Jung: Analyst creates therapy nearer art than science. *New York Times* (July 2): C1, C8.

Golin, M. 1988. Tapping your "Wise Man" within. *Prevention* (May): 65–68.

Gordon, H. 1987. *Extrasensory deception.* Buffalo, N.Y.: Prometheus Books.

———. 1988. Thinking and the paranormal. *Free Inquiry* 8(3): 15–16.

Gordon, J. S. 1987. *The golden guru.* Lexington, Mass.: Stephen Greene Press.

Gould, S. J. 1987–88. The verdict on creationism. *The Skeptical Inquirer* 12(2): 184–187.

Granger, P. 1972. Humanistic and transpersonal psychology: Similarities and differences. *Association for Humanistic Psychology Newsletter* 8(5): 21–22.

Grant, E. 1988. Scientology's honcho. Review of *L. Ron Hubbard: Madman or Messiah?* by Bent Corydon and L. Ron Hubbard, Jr. *Psychology Today* (July): 79.

Greeley, A. 1987. Mysticism goes mainstream. *American Health* (January): 47–49.

Grieger, R., and Boyd, J. 1980. *Rational-emotive therapy: A skills based approach.* New York: Van Nostrand Reinhold.

Grieger, R., and Grieger, I. Z. 1982. *Cognition and emotional disturbance.* New York: Human Sciences Press.

Griffin, N. 1984. Bertrand Russell's crisis of faith. *Russell* 4(1): 101–122.

Grof, S., ed. 1984. *Ancient wisdom and modern science.* Stony Brook, N.Y.: State University of New York Press.

Grof, S., and Grof, C. 1988. The transpersonal perspective. *Association for Humanistic Psychology Perspective* (May): 4.

Gross, J. 1987. Review of *Holy terror* by Amir Taheri. *New York Times* (November): 11, C17.

Gruson, L. 1985. Key witness in trial in L. I. describes ritualistic killing. *New York Times* (April 10): B4.

———. 1986a. Friction over Krishnas in West Virginia's hills. *New York Times* (October 1): A18.

———. 1986. Murder jury told of sect intrigues. *New York Times* (December 3): A21.

Guru's Book Is Burned at Oregon Commune. 1985. *New York Times* (October 1): A15.

Gusic, D. B. 1988. A course in miracles. *New York Open Center Catalogue* (May): 31.

Gutsch, K. U., Sisemore, D. A., and Williams, R. L. 1984. *Systems of psychotherapy.* Springfield, Ill.: Thomas.

Haberman, C. 1986. Modern Japan, land of superstition. *New York Times* (July 7): A3.

Hadden, J. K., and Shupe, A. 1988. *Televangelism.* New York: Holt.

Hamburg, D. A. 1986. New risks, ethnocentrism, and violence. *Science* 231: 533.

Hammer, M. 1971. Quiet mind therapy. *Voices* 1(1): 52–56.

Hansel, C. E. M. 1980. *ESP and parapsychology: A critical reevaluation.* Buffalo, N,Y,: Prometheus Books.

———. 1984. The evidence for ESP: A critique. *The Skeptical Inquirer* 8: 322–328.

Harman, W. 1983 [1981]. Science and the clarification of values. *Journal of Humanistic Psychology* 21(3): 3–16.

———. 1985. Firewalk for peace. *Association for Humanistic Psychology Harm Perspective* (December): 16–17.

Harper, R. A. 1983. Letter to editor on prayer. *Newsletter of the American Academy of Psychotherapists* 1.

Harris, B. 1987. *Gellerism revealed.* Seattle, Wash.: Micky Hades International.

Harris, L. 1985. *Holy days.* New York: Summit Books. Reviewed in the *New York Times Book Review* (November 10): 9–11.

Hauck, P. 1973. *Overcoming depression.* Philadelphia: Westminster.

———. 1974. *Overcoming frustration and anger.* Philadelphia: Westminster.

———. 1975. *Overcoming worry and fear.* Philadelphia: Westminster.

———. 1979. *Brief counseling with RET.* Philadelphia: Westminster.

Hazarika, S. 1984. 574 Sikh deserters reportedly held by Indian forces. *New York Times* (June 12): A1, A6.

Heesacker, M., Heppner, P., and Rogers, M. 1982. Classics and emerging classics in counseling psychology. *Journal of Counseling Psychology* 29: 400–405.

Hendlin, S. T. 1982. Quieting the mind through meditation. *Voices* 17(4): 55–60.

Hijazi, I. A. 1985. One thousand Shiites rally at Beirut airport. *New York Times* (June 21): 1, 4.

———. 1986a. Syrian troops start patrols in Shiite outskirts of Beirut. *New York Times* (August 5): A3.

———. 1986b. Lebanon kidnappers deny reports of secret messages. *New York Times* (August 31): A3.

———. 1988. Syria says Iran is in accord on troops in Beirut suburbs. *New York Times National Edition* (May 27): 5.

Hines, T. 1988. *Pseudoscience and the paranormal: A critical examination of the evidence.* Buffalo, N.Y.: Prometheus Books.

Hobbs, C. 1988. Superimmunity: Herbs and other natural remedies for a healthy immune system. *Joy Lake Mountain Center Catalogue of Events,* 18.

Hock, R. A. 1983. A Teilhardian mass: Liturgy for participating in evolution. *Journal of Humanistic Psychology* 23(4): 7–24.

Hon, S. 1985. Healing calligraphy. *New York Open Center Catalogue* (May-August): 15.

Houdini, H. 1924. *A magician among the spirits.* New York: Harper & Row.

Houdini, H., and Dunninger, J. 1947. *Magic and mystery.* New York: Weathervane Books.

Houston, J. 1982. *The possible human.* Los Angeles: Tarcher.

Howell, A. D. 1988. Astrology, Jung and psychotherapy. August workshop. *Saratoga Summer Symposia,* 4.

Hunt, D., and McMahon, T. A. 1985. *The seduction of Christianity.* Eugene, Oreg.: Harvest House Publishers.

Inmate Said to Lead Cult Mixing Sex and Religion. 1983. *New York Times* (December 4): A16.

Johnsen, S., and Benedetti, A. 1984. Rebirthing and spiritual purification training. *Gathering of the Ways* (Summer): 6.

Kahane, M. 1985. Yes, by liberal Jews. *New York Times* (December 20): A35.

Kamm, H. 1985. 2 gunmen kill 21 in synagogue; bar doors and then open fire at Sabbath service in Istanbul. *New York Times* (September 7): A1, A12.

Kaslow, F., and Sussman, M. B., eds. 1985. *Cults and the family.* New York: Haworth.

Katz, B. 1985. Rationality speaking. *The American Rationalist* 29: 87.

Katz, R. 1982. *Boiling energy: Community healing among the Kalahari Kung.* Cambridge, Mass.: Harvard University Press.

Kazdin, A. E. 1978. *History of behavior modification: Experimental foundations of contemporary research.* Baltimore, Md.: University Park Press.

Kazdin, A. E., & Wilson, G. T. 1978. *Evaluation of behavior therapy: Issues, evidence and research strategies.* Cambridge, Mass.: Ballinger.

Keller, B. 1988. The Russians, too, embrace "secret silliness" of astrology. *New York Times* (May 16): 1, 4.

Kelly, J., and Domville, E., eds. 1986. *The collected letters of W. B. Yeats.* New York: Oxford.

Keppe, N. R. 1983. The right path. *Trilogy* 1(4): 9.

Khomeini, A. 1985. Quoted in *Harper's Magazine* (August).

Kifner, J. 1985a. Bombing in Beirut has troubling echoes. *New York Times* (May 19): E5.

———. 1985b. Hostages linked to Lebanese clan. *New York Times* (August 1): A1, A4.

———. 1988. With the Afghan guerrillas in a heady time. *New York Times National Edition* (May 27): 1, 5.

King, W. 1985. Anti-Semitism links violent groups. *New York Times* (April 28): A22.

———. 1988. Man charged in plot on Jackson suggested others were involved. *New York Times* (May 19): A1, B12.

Kinsbourne, M. 1982. Hemispheric specialization and the growth of human understanding. *American Psychologist* 37: 411–420.

Kinzer, S. 1987. In the country of the occult, power to the spirits. *New York Times* (June 9): 64.

Klass, P. J. 1986. The Condon UFO study: A trick or a conspiracy? *The Skeptical Inquirer* 10(4): 328–341.

Klerman, G. L., Rounsville, B., Chevron, E., Neu, C., and Weissman, M. 1979. *Manual for short-term interpersonal psychother-*

apy (IPT) of depression. New Haven: Boston Collaborative Depression Project.

Komaki, H. 1984. *Eternal happiness of all spiritual beings of the infinite universe.* Santa Monica, Calif.: Komaki Foundation.

Korzybski, A. 1933. *Science and sanity.* San Francisco: International Society for General Semantics.

Kostelanetz, R. 1984. The distinctions of humanism. *Free Inquiry* 4(2): 47.

Krippner, S. 1981. Herbs and healers: A recommendation. *Association for Humanistic Psychology Newsletter* (January): 6.

————. 1984. The Randi caper. *Association for Humanistic Psychology Newsletter* (July): 20–21.

————. 1986. Cross-cultural approaches to multiple personality: Therapeutic practices in Brazilian spiritism. *Humanistic Psychologist* 14(2): 176–93.

Kuhn, T. S. 1970. *The structure of scientific revolutions.* Chicago: University of Chicago Press.

Kurtz, P. 1985a. *A skeptic's handbook of parapsychology.* Buffalo, N.Y.: Prometheus Books.

————. 1985b. Finding a common ground between believers and unbelievers. *Free Inquiry* 5(3): 10–12.

————. 1986a. *The transcendental temptation: A critique of religion and the paranormal.* Buffalo, N.Y.: Prometheus Books.

————. 1986b. Does faith-healing work? *Free Inquiry* 6(2): 30–36.

————. 1986c. W. V. Grant's faith-healing act revisited. *Free Inquiry* 6(3): 12–13.

Kurtz, P., Alcock, J., Frazier, K., Karr, B., Klass, P. J., and Randi, J. 1988. Testing psi claims in China: Visit by a CSICOP delegation. *The Skeptical Inquirer* 12: 364–85.

Lacey, L. A. 1982. *Effective communication with difficult people.* San Diego: Common Visions.

Lange, A., and Jakubowski, P. 1976. *Responsible assertive behavior.* Champaigne, Ill.: Research Press.

Lasch, C. 1978. *The culture of narcissism.* New York: Norton.

Laskow, L. 1988. Deepening healing abilities with transformational energies. *Joy Lake Mountain Center Catalogue of Events,* 16.

Laurence, T. 1974. *Satan, sorcery and sex.* West Nyack, N.Y.: Parker Publishing Co.

LaVey, A. Z. 1972. *The satanic rituals.* Secaucus, N.J.: University Books.

Lazarus, A. A. 1977. Toward an egoless state of being. In *Handbook of rational-emotive therapy,* edited by A. Ellis and R. Grieger, vol. I, 113–116. New York: Springer.

Leahey, T. H., and Leahey, G. E. 1983. *Psychology's occult doubles.* Chicago: Nelson Hall.

Leake, C. D. 1973. State-specific sciences. *Science* 180: 1005.

Leikind, B. J., and McCarthy, W. J. 1985. An investigation of firewalking. *The Skeptical Inquirer* 16(1): 23–24.

Leonard, G. B. 1972. *The transformation.* New York: Delacorte.

Lerner, M. 1986. The unraveling of a guru's dream. *Insight* (April 21): 72–74.

LeShan, L. 1984. *From Newton to ESP.* New York: Turnstone Press.

Lesser, W. 1984. Review of *The fire from within* by Carlos Castenada. *New York Times Book Review* (June 10): 27.

Lester, D., Thinschmidt, J. S., and Trautman, L. A. 1987. Paranormal belief and Jungian dimensions of personality. *Psychological Reports* 61: 182.

Levine, S. L. 1984. Radical departures. *Psychology Today* 18(8): 12–27.

Levinthal, C. 1983. *Introduction to physiological psychology.* Englewood Cliffs, N.J.: Prentice-Hall, Inc.

Levy, J. 1983. Transpersonal psychology and Jungian psychology. *Journal of Humanistic Psychology* 23(2): 42–51.

Lewin, T. 1988a. When it's one absolute right against another. *New York Times* (May 29): F16.

———. 1988. Custody case lifts veil on a "psychotherapy cult." *New York Times* (June 3): B1–2.

Lewinsohn, P. A. 1974. Behavioral approach to depression. In *The Psychology of depression,* edited by R. Friedman and M. Katz. Washington, D.C.: Winston.

Lewis, A. 1984. The righteous fanatics. *New York Times* (September 27): A23.

Lindsey, R. 1984. Scientology chief got millions, ex-aides say. *New York Times* (July 11): A1, A21.

———. 1986a. L. Ron Hubbard dies of stroke, founder of Scientology. *New York Times* (January 29): 29.

———. 1986b. Spiritual concepts drawing a different breed of adherents. *New York Times* (September 29): A1, B12.

———. 1987. Spiritual games: A growing fad. *New York Times* (May 12): A16.

Londer, R. 1985. Cure by diet? *Health* 17(10): 54–55.

Luce, G., and Hudak, M. R. 1986. Introduction to the mystical body of Christ. *Joy Lake Mountain Center Catalogue,* 25.

Luce, J. D. 1986. The fundamentalists' anonymous movement. *The Humanist* 46(1): 11–12, 36.

Luttwak, E. N. 1984. Inviting terror. *New York Times* (August 15): A23.

McAleavy, D. 1983. The lesson of Jonestown. *American Atheist* 25 (11): 20.

McCorkle, L. 1969. *How to make love.* New York: Grove Press.

McDermott, R. B. 1986. The human cycle: From birth to death according to Rudolf Steiner. *New York Open Center Catalogue* (September): 28.

MacDougall, C. D. 1983. *Superstition and the press.* Buffalo, N.Y.: Prometheus Books.

McFadden, R. D. 1984. Youth found hanged in Long Island cell after his arrest in ritual killing. *New York Times* (July 8): 1, 20.

―――. 1985. Israelis believe pro-Libya group raided airports. *New York Times* (December 30): A1, A8.

Mackenzie, R. 1986. Iran's hell on earth for Iraqi's POWs. *Insight* (April 21): 35.

McMahon, W., and Griffis, J. 1986. Further reflections on Ernest Angley. *Free Inquiry* 6(3): 15–17.

Madagascar kills twenty in a sect. 1985. *New York Times* (August 3): 3.

Maharishi Mahesh Yogi. 1982. Maharishi's message to every government. *New York Times* (July 28): A14.

―――. 1983a. Governments invited. *New York Times* (October 10): A14.

―――. 1983b. Maharishi technology of a unified field. *New York Times* (December 12): B20.

Mahoney, M. J. 1974. *Cognition and behavior modification.* Cambridge, Mass.: Ballinger.

Malcolm, A. H. 1984. Iowa town contemplates pitfalls of being mediators' utopia. *New York Times* (January 1): 14.

Mann, R. D. 1984. *The light of consciousness: Explorations in transpersonal psychology.* Albany, N.Y.: State University of New York Press.

Matthiessen, P. 1986. Nine-headed dragon river: Zen journals 1969–1985. *New York Times Book Review* (April 6): 23.

Maultsby, M. C., Jr., and Ellis, A. 1974. *Technique of using rational-emotive imagery.* New York: Institute for Rational-Emotive Therapy.

May, C. D. 1984a. Religion and kinship still cut deeply in Africa. *New York Times* (May 27): E3.

―――. 1984b. Religious frictions heat up in Nigeria. *New York Times* (August 12): E2.

May, R. 1986. Transpersonal psychology. *APA Monitor* 17(5): 2.

Mehl, L. 1986. The healing ways of Native American spirituality. *New York Open Center Catalogue* (September): 8.

Meichenbaum, D. 1977. *Cognitive-behavioral modification.* New York: Plenum.

Menendez, A. J. 1984. On canonizing Reagan. *Church and State* 37(5): 19–20.

Michael, D. N. 1985. Aquarians riding the third wave. *Journal of Humanistic Psychology* 25(1): 79–84.

Miller, J. 1986. World terrorism: A report to NATO paints a dark picture. *New York Times* (November 14): A10.

Milne, H. 1987. *Bhagwan: The god that failed.* New York: St. Martin's Press.

Mishlove, J. 1983. *Psi development systems.* Jefferson, N.C.: McFarland.

Monetathchi, E. 1988. *Workshop on traditional Indian medicine.* July 29 to August 5. Tucson, Arizona.

Montgomery, R. 1985. *Aliens among us.* New York: Putnam.

Montgomery, R., and Garland, J. 1986. *Ruth Montgomery: Herald of the new age.* New York: Dolphin/Doubleday.

Morain, L. 1988. How pseudoscientists get away with it. *The Humanist* 48(2): 17–22, 30.

Mormon Professor Faces Furor at Baptist University. 1984. *New York Times* (July 8): 30.

Moss, C. M., and Hosford, R. E. 1983. Reflections on EST training from two correctional psychologists. *International Journal of Eclectic Psychotherapy* 2(1): 18–39.

Mountain Group Linked to Murder. 1985. *New York Times* (April 25): B19.

Nathan, S. 1985. Russell's scientific mysticism. *Russell* 5(1): 14–25.

Neese, L. H. 1984. The humanistic challenge to traditional religions. *The Humanist* 44(4): 17–20.

Negri, M. 1984. Why biblical criticism by scholars is imperative. *The Humanist* 44(3): 27–28.

———. 1988. Age-old problems of the new age movement. *The Humanist* 48(2): 23–26.

Neher, A. 1980. *The psychology of transcendence.* Englewood Cliffs, N.J.: Prentice-Hall.

Nickell, J. 1987. *Inquest on the Shroud of Turin.* Buffalo, N.Y.: Prometheus Books.

O'Hara, M. 1983. A hundredth monkey myth. *Association for Humanistic Psychology Newsletter* (November): 20–21.

Ohta, T. 1983. Focusing: A psychological method where the East and West meet. *Focusing Folio* 2(4): 1–10.

Osborne, J. W., and Baldwin J. R. 1982. Psychotherapy: From one state of illusion to another. *Psychotherapy* 19: 266–274.

Parsons, R. D., and Wicks, R. J. 1986. Cognitive pastoral psychotherapy with religious persons experiencing loneliness. *The Psychotherapy Patient* 2(3): 47–59.

Peck, M. S. 1983. *People of the lie?* New York: Simon & Schuster.

Pennachio, J. 1983. Symbols and the lost unity of human experience. *Etc.* 40(1): 59–74.

Pinker, S. 1987. Deviations from normality. *Contemporary Psychology* 32: 806–807.

Plasil, E. 1985. *Therapist.* New York: St. Martin's/Marek.

Popper, K. R. 1985. *Popper selections.* Princeton, N.J.: Princeton University Press.

Prabhupada, A. C. B. 1977. *The science of self realization.* Los Angeles, Calif.: The Bhaktivedanta Book Trust.

Questions and Answers on Basics 1986. *Seikyo Times* (November): 26–40.

Rachleff, O. W. 1971. *The occult conceit.* New York: Bell Publishing Co.

Radical Right Tills the Heartland. 1985. *Insight* 1(14): 24–26.

Rajneesh haven: A legacy of debts. 1988. *New York Times* (April 24): A41.

Raloff, J. 1984. Building the ultimate weapons. *Science News* 126: 42–45.

Rama, Sri Swami. 1982. Karma is the maker. *Himalayan News* (September/October): 3.

Randi, J. 1986a. "Be healed in the name of God!" An expose of the Reverend W. V. Grant. *Free Inquiry* 6(12): 8–20.

———. 1986b. Peter Popoff reaches heaven via 39.17 Megahertz. *Free Inquiry* 6(3): 6–7.

———. 1987. *The Faith Healers.* Buffalo, N.Y.: Prometheus Books.

Randi, J., and USA Today 1986. Magic's to entertain; it's not for swindling. *USA Today* (August 24): 9A.

Raphael, D. 1982. That therapeutic touch. *East Side Express* (August 12): 5.

Rawcliffe, D. H. 1952. *Occult and supernatural phenomena.* New York: Dover.

Ray, S., and Lehrman, F. 1984. The first god training: Advanced course in spiritual mastery. *Gathering of the Ways* (Summer): 10.

Read, A. W. 1983. The place of "mysticism" and "occultism" in the scientific orientation. *The Humanist* 43(5): 12–13, 46.

Regan, D. T. 1988. *For the record.* New York: Harcourt Brace Jovanovich.

Rensberger, B. 1974. False tests peril psychic research. *New York Times* (August 20): 14.

Restivo, S. 1983. *The social relations of physics, mysticism, and mathematics.* Hingham, Mass.: Reidel Publications.

Rice, B. 1980. Mind bending at Berkeley. *Psychology Today* 14(5): 8–12.

Rimm, D. C., and Masters, J. C. 1979. *Behavior therapy: Techniques and empirical findings.* New York: Academic Press.

Rinpoche, C. T. 1986. P'Howa: The transference of consciousness at the moment of death. *Joy Lake Mountain Seminar Center Catalogue,* 13.

———. 1988. The chod healing ceremony. *Joy Lake Mountain Center Catalogue of Events,* 13.

Risenberg, H. 1982. Practical applications of psychic phenomena in psychotherapy. *Association for Humanistic Psychology Newsletter* (August): 22–23.

Ritscher, H. J. 1985. Henry George and Rudolf Steiner. *Fragments* 43(1–2): i.

Roberts, J. 1979. *The "unknown" reality: A Seth book.* Vol. 2. Englewood Cliffs, N.J.: Prentice-Hall.

Roberts, S. V. 1988a. Astrology quiz: Will the Reagans hurt business? *New York Times* (May 1): B1.

———. 1988b. White House confirms Reagans follow astrology, up to a point. *New York Times* (May 4): A1, B9.

Roberts, T. B. 1982. Comment on Mathes's article. *Journal of Humanistic Psychology* 22(4): 97–98.

Rockwell, J. 1984a. Philharmonic replaces work by Bloch at Malaysia request. *New York Times* (August 10): C1, C4.

———. 1984b. No Malaysia visit for philharmonic. *New York Times* (August 11): 1, 12.

Roelofsma, D. K. 1986. A frenzied tattoo of violence. *Insight* 1(15): 44–45.

———. 1987. Inside the circle of witches modern. *Insight* 3(23): 59–61.

Rogers, C. R. 1961. *On becoming a person.* Boston, Mass.: Houghton-Mifflin.

———. 1980. *A way of being.* Boston, Mass.: Houghton-Mifflin.

Rorer, L. G. 1988. Rational-emotive theory: 1. An integrated psychological and philosophical basis. Unpublished manuscript, Miami University, Oxford, Ohio.

Rosenthal, A. M. 1988. This censored world. *New York Times National Edition* (May 27): 23.

Rosicrucians. 1984. He has inner vision. *New York Times* (June 3): 44.

———. 1985. *The mastery of life.* San Jose, Calif.: Supreme Grand Lodge of Ancient and Mystical Order of Rosicrucians.

Rotton, J. 1985. Astrological forecasts and the commodity market: Random walks as a source of illusory correlation. *The Skeptical Inquirer* 9(4): 339–346.

Rowan, J. 1987. Nine humanistic heresies. *Journal of Humanistic Psychology* 7(2): 141–157.

———. 1988. Therapist blocking: A common problem? *Association for Humanistic Psychology Perspective* (May): 7.

Russell, B. 1965. *The basic writings of Bertrand Russell.* New York: Simon & Schuster.

Russell, P. 1986. Beware the firewalk. *Association for Humanistic Psychology Perspective* (March): 6.

Sacks, O. 1985. *Migraine: Understanding a common disorder.* Berkeley, Calif.: University of Berkeley Press.

Safavi, A. 1986. Ending Khomeini's blood bath. *New York Times* (October 1): A27.

Sagan, C. 1987. The burden of skepticism. *The Skeptical Inquirer* 12(1): 38–46.

Sartre, J.-P. 1968. *Being and nothingness.* New York: Washington Square Press.

Savan, L. 1986. Consider the alternatives: Vitamins and crystals, homeopathy and herbs. *Village Voice* (May 27): 25–27.

Saxon, W. 1983. Ruth Carter Stapleton dies: Evangelist and faith healer. *New York Times* (September 27): D32.

Schafersman, S. 1986. Peter Popoff: Miracle worker or scam artist? *Free Inquiry* 6(3): 8–9.

Schell, J. 1982. *The fate of the earth.* New York: Knopf.

———. 1984. *The abolition.* New York: Knopf.

Scherling, R. 1984. Colonic irrigation. *Gathering of the Ways Catalogue* (Summer): 14.

Schneider, K. 1987. The deified self: A "centaur" response to Wilber and the transpersonal movement. *Journal of Humanistic Psychology* 17: 196–216.

Schumacher, E. 1984. Chile's leader belittles foes, vows to stay on. *New York Times* (August 8): A1, A4.

Scott, W. 1970. *Demonology and witchcraft.* New York: Bell Publishing Co.

Seckel, A. 1986–87. Science, creationism, and the U.S. Supreme Court. *The Skeptical Inquirer* 11(2): 147–158.

Secunda, B. 1988. Spirit of the heart: The healing way of Huichol shamanism. *Joy Lake Mountain Center Catalogue of Events,* 28.

Shah, I. 1982. *The Sufis.* London: Octagon Press.

Shapiro, D. H., and Walsh, R. N., eds. 1984. *Meditation: Classic and contemporary perspectives.* New York: Aldine.

Shelburne, W. A. 1987. Carlos Castaneda: If it didn't happen, what does it matter? *Journal of Humanistic Psychology* 27(2): 217–27.

Shinnah, O. 1988. The therapeutic use of crystals and gemstones. Joy Lake Mountain Center Catalogue of Events, 26.

Sichel, J., and Ellis, A. 1983. *RET self-help report form.* New York Institute for Rational-Emotive Therapy.

Silva J., amd Miehle, P. 1977. *The Silva mind control method.* New York: Simon & Schuster

Silva Mind Control. 1984. Advertisement. *Landmark* 11(1): 4–5.

Simons, M. 1986. Voodoo under attack in post-Duvalier Haiti. *New York Times* (May 15): A1, A12.

Singer, P. 1986. A medical anthropologist's view of American shamans. *Free Inquiry* 6(2): 20–23.

Skutel, H. J. 1984. Talmudic fundamentalism and the Arab-Israeli conflict. *American Atheist* 26(6): 17–20.

Smerlin, T. 1985. Yes, by Kahanism. *New York Times* (December 20): A35.

Smith, D. 1982. Trends in counseling and psychotherapy. *American Psychologist,* 37, 802–809.

Smith, G. H. 1979. Atheism: The case against God. Buffalo, N.Y.: Prometheus Books.

Smith, T. 1984. Iran: Five years of fanatacism. *New York Times Magazine* (February 12): 20–34.

Smothers, R. 1988. In a small southern town, a church and child welfare officials do battle. *New York Times* (June 11): A16.

Sobel, H. J. 1981. *Behavior therapy in terminal care: A humanistic approach.* Cambridge, Mass.: Ballinger.

Sobran, J. 1984. Religion comes first. *New York Times* (August 12): E21.

Spirit Speaks. 1985. Los Angeles: Spirit Speaks.

Stace, W. T. 1960. *The teachings of the mystics.* New York: New American Library.

Stalker, D., and Glymour, C. 1985. *Examining holistic medicine.* Buffalo, N.Y.: Prometheus Books.

Stark, E. 1984. Not-so-skeptical inquirers. *Psychology Today* (September): 76.

Starr, D. 1984. The crying need for a believable theology. *The Humanist* 44(4): 13–16, 50.

Stein, M. 1987. Fundamentalists: Notes on a personality analysis and religiosity as neurosis. *American Atheist* 29(12): 13–15.

Steiner, R. A. 1986. Behind the scenes with Peter Popoff. *Free Inquiry* 6(3): 10–11.

Stevens, P., Jr. 1988. The appeal of the occult: Some thoughts on history, religion and science. *The Skeptical Inquirer* 12: 376–385.

Suchman, H., and Thetford, W. 1975. *A course in miracles.* Tiburon, Calif.: Foundation for Inner Peace.

Sullivan, R. 1988. Steinberg companion willing to testify in girl's death. *New York Times* (May 9): B1, B4.

Sundberg, N. D., and Tyler, C. E. 1962. *Clinical psychology.* New York: Appleton-Century-Crofts.

Suzuki, D. T., Fromm, E., and DeMartino, R. 1963. *Zen Buddhism and psychoanalysis.* New York: Grove Press.

Svoboda, R. 1988. Ayurvedic medicine. *New York Open Center Catalogue* (May/September): 23.

Szymusiak, C. 1985. Vipassana. *Meditation* (Winter): 6–8, 33.

Tagliabue, J. 1985. Airport terrorists kill 13 and wound 113 at Israeli counters in Rome and Vienna. *New York Times* (December 28): 1, 4.

Taheri, A. 1987. *Holy terror.* New York: Adler and Adler.

Tannous, A. I. 1983. On aggression and cooperation. *Association for Humanistic Psychology Newsletter* (November): 25.

Tart, C. T., ed. 1975. *Transpersonal psychologies.* New York: Harper Colophon Books.

———. 1988. Growing wise hearts, bodies and minds. *AHP Perspective* (May): 5.

Ten Racists Are Convicted on Racketeering Charges by Seattle Jury. 1985. *New York Times* (December 31): 7.

Tester, S. J. 1984. *A history of western astrology.* Wolfeboro, N.H.: Boydell & Brewer.

Thirteen Synanon Members Answer an Indictment. 1984. *New York Times* (July 11): A21.

Thirty-five Reported Killed in New India Riots. 1984. *New York Times* (May 24): A3.

Thomsen, D. E. 1983. A knowing universe seeking to be known. *Science News* 123: 124.

Tulku, T. 1977. *Gesture of Balance.* Berkeley, Calif.: Dharma.

———. 1988. *Openness of mind.* Berkeley, Calif.: Dharma.

Two in Sect Charged in Insurance Case. 1987. *New York Times* (September 18): B5.

Ullman, D. 1988. Getting past wellness macho. *Association for Humanistic Psychology Perspective* (June): 4.

Valle, R. S. 1986. Transpersonal psychology: A reply to Rollo May. *The Humanistic Psychologist* 14(3): 210–13.

van den Hart, O. 1983. *Rituals in psychotherapy: Transition and continuity.* New York: Irvington.

Venn, J. 1988. Hypnosis and reincarnation. A critique and case study. *The Skeptical Inquirer* 12: 386–92.

Viloldo, A. 1986. The shaman's journey. Workshop. *Northwest Regional AHP Conference,* Detroit, Oreg., September, 1986.

Walen, S. R., DiGiuseppe, R., and Wessler, R. L. 1980. *A practitioner's guide to rational-emotive therapy.* New York: Oxford.

Walsh, R. 1982. The world view of Ken Wilber. *Association for Humanistic Psychology Newsletter* (May): 4–7.

Walsh, R., and Vaughan, F. 1988. Transpersonal psychology: A synoptic overview. *Association for Humanistic Perspective* (May): 4.

Warnke, P. C. 1984. Review of *The abolition* by Jonathan Schell. *New York Times Book Review* (July 8): 8–9.

Watson, J. B. 1919. *Psychology from the standpoint of a behaviorist.* Philadelphia, Pa.: Lippincott.

Watts, A. 1982. *Play to live.* San Francisco, Calif.: And Books.

Weber, E. 1985. Power from the barrel of a gun. *New York Times Book Review* (November 17): 13–14.

Weed, S. 1988. Green witch week. *Joy Lake Mountain Center Catalogue of Events,* 23.

Weinrach, S. G. 1980. Unconventional therapist: Albert Ellis. *Personnel and Guidance Journal* 59: 152–160.

Weisman, S. R. 1986a. Three are killed and 500 arrested in Sikh protests in the Punjab. *New York Times* (January 1): 2.

———. 1986b. A pilgrim's progress ends on Ganges. *New York Times* (April 19): 2.

———. 1988. Two bombs in shopping area kill 24. *New York Times* (June 22): A9.

Werner, L. M. 1984. Synanon rejected on its tax appeal. *New York Times* (February 10): A12.

Wessler, R. A., and Wessler, R. A. 1980. *The principle and practice of rational-emotive therapy.* San Francisco, Calif.: Jossey-Bass.

White, S. E. 1987. *The Betty book.* Columbus, Ohio: Ariel Press.

Wiener, D. 1988. *Albert Ellis: Passionate skeptic.* New York: Praeger.

Wilber, K. 1982a. *A sociable god.* New York: McGraw-Hill.

———. 1982b. In defense of Descartes. *Association of Humanistic Psychology Newsletter:* 7–9.

———. 1982c. The pre/trans fallacy. *Journal of Humanistic Psychology* 22(2): 5–43.

———. (in press). Let's nuke the transpersonalists. *Journal of Counseling and Development.*

Wilczek, F., and Devine, B. 1988. *Longing for the harmonies: Themes and variations from modern physics.* New York: Norton.

Wilson, I. 1982. *Reincarnation? The claims investigated.* New York: Penguin Books.

Witkin, G. 1985. Applications of rational-emotive therapy to health practice. In *Clinical applications of rational-emotive therapy,* edited by A. Ellis and M. E. Bernard. New York: Plenum.

Wolkomir, R. 1984. Do you hear what I'm thinking? *American Way* 17(4): 46–48.

Woolger, R. 1986. Other lives, other selves: A Jungian approach to past life therapy. *New York Open Center Catalogue* (September): 17.

Wien, C. S. 1986. Filipino Moslems: A new piece to put in the puzzle. *New York Times* (May 13): A2.

Wrobel, A., ed. 1987. *Pseudo-science and society in nineteenth-century America.* Lexington, Ky.: University of Kentucky Press.

Wykert, J. 1975. The guru and his followers. *Psychiatric News* (July 16): 1, 28.

Yale, M, 1984. The way we think. *The Humanist* 44(4): 21–22, 38.

Yamamoto, K. 1988. Katsugen natural movement. *New York Open Center Catalogue* (May/September): 4.

Yates, S. A. 1986. Seeds of hate in Coeur d'Alene. *USA Today* 9A.

Yeats, W. B. 1986. *The collected letters of W. B. Yeats.* New York: Oxford.

Zindler, F. R. 1988. Religiosity as a mental disease. *American Atheist.* Hillsdale, N.J.: Erlbaum.